The Women's Heritage Scrapbook

by
Susannah Hay

Caillech Press
St. Paul MN

Published in the United States by Caillech Press, 482 Michigan Street, St. Paul Minnesota 55102.

Printed by Kaye's Printing, Fargo, North Dakota.

ISBN 0-9624836-8-0

First Edition

Cover illustration from the collection of the National Archives, Washington, DC; #83-G-41089

Table of Contents

A Note to the Reader

Today we know so much about women's achievements that a book like this one is difficult to write. Women's studies is one of the most exciting and most rapidly-expanding areas of contemporary scholarship. Thousands of books now sit on library shelves where there were none a generation ago. The comparative wealth of information makes writing capsule summaries difficult.

The Women's Heritage Scrapbook describes some of what we now know about notable individual women. You'll find few contemporary women here--I've focused on people who are noteworthy for a body of work over a lifetime. Age may not correlate with achievement: athletes complete a career at 40 or even 25, while scientists and others continue into old age. In every field, the list of notables could be lengthened considerably.

I've attempted to provide a sense of global participation, while emphasizing American women. Much more is available to English-speaking researchers on women in Western culture, of course. One does yearn to be able to read many languages when faced with the paucity of information about Asian and Middle Eastern women, particularly.

Walk into history in the company of women! It is not enough to read a few sentences about an accomplished women--it is more important(and fun) to experience history, literature, art or travel. The listings of landmarks, monuments, museums and films are your first steps in retracing and revisiting the lives of pioneers and legends. *Sources for Further Reading* allows you to explore individual women or certain field in much greater depth.

A note about terms: I dislike the practice of labelling white American people "American" and people of color "African-" or "Hispanic-American." This text initially used "Euro-American," but I came to the conclusion that the term was too vague; it probably is misleading for many whites. So I have provided information about ethnicity or racial heritage when available. Otherwise, I have noted the country each woman lived in.

The Scrapbook was designed to accommodate hand-written additional notes. Please take advantage of the blank spaces to make this book truly your own.

Thanks to Judy Voshell and Gwen Welckle for their support and assistance with editing and composition.

Susannah Hay
August, 1992

She speaks to the ten greatest American women:
The anonymous farmer's wife, the anonymous clubbed picket,
the anonymous Negro woman who held off the guns,
the anonymous prisoner, anonymous cotton-picker
trailing her robe of sack in a proud train,
anonymous writer of these and mill-hand, anonymous city-walker,
anonymous organizer, anonymous binder of the illegally wounded,
anonymous feeder and speaker to anonymous squares.
She knows their faces, their impatient songs
of passionate grief risen, the desperate music
poverty makes, she knows women cut down
by poverty, by stupid obscure days,
their moments over the dishes, speaks them now,
wrecks with the whole necessity of the past
behind the debris, behind the ordinary
smell of coffee, the ravelling clean wash,
the turning to bed, undone among savage night
planning and unplanning seasons of happiness
broken in dreams or in the jaundiced morning
over a tub or over a loom or over
the tired face of death.

Muriel Rukeyser
From *"Ann Burlak"*

❝ *I long to speak out the intense inspiration that comes to me*
*from the lives of strong women.***❞**

Ruth Benedict
Letter, 1917

Art
&
Architecture

❝ I grew up pretty much as everybody else grows up, and one day . . .
found myself saying to myself--I can't live where I want to--I can't go
where I want to--I can't do what I want to--I can't even say what I want to--
School and things that painters have taught me even keep me from painting as I want to.
I decided I was a very stupid fool not to at least paint as I wanted to and say
what I wanted to when I painted as that seemed to be the only thing
I can do that didn't concern anybody but myself--
that was nobody's business but my own. ❞
Georgia O'Keeffe*

❝ Conformity and monotony, even when they are embellished with a froth of novelty,
are not attributes of developing and economically vigorous cities.
They are attributes of stagnant settlements. ❞
Jane Jacobs*
The Economy of Cities, 1969

Painters

Few names of either sex have survived of the artists in ancient times.
Now, over 200 female artists are known to us in the 17th century alone.

Sofonisba Anguissola (c.1532-1625)
Italian. The first internationally-known female artist, an inventive Renaissance portraitist, and a role model for many women of her time.

Artemisia Gentileschi* (1593-c.1652)
Italian. Baroque painter among the best of her generation, known for her vigorous personal style in religious paintings(*Susanna and the Elders*).

Louise Moillon (1610-1696)
French. A pioneer in French still life painting. Her superb sense of composition and lush color are used in an elegant, restrained manner.

Judith Leyster* (1609-1660)
Dutch. A major 17th-century portrait painter significant for her unorthodox approach to popular themes.

Rosalba Carriera* (1675-1757)
Italian(Venetian). Accomplished, innovative painter who was elected to both Italian and French academies. She invented the pastel portrait(using colored chalk) and was the first to use ivory as the "canvas" for miniature portraits.

Angelica Kauffman* (1741-1807)
Swiss-born Briton. One of two female founding members of the British Royal Academy and a painter of historical subjects, an unusual category for women at that time. Among the most highly-respected artists of her era.

Marie-Louise-Elisabeth Vigée LeBrun (1755-1842)
French. Court painter of vibrant portraits, who became one of the foremost painters of the time. Her sponsor was Marie-Antoinette.

Lilly Martin Spencer* (1822-1902)
French-American. An important Victorian painter especially successful with humorous domestic subjects. She designed many paintings for reproduction in magazines of the day.

Rosa Bonheur* (1822-1899)
French. She was called the "world's greatest animal painter" in the Western world during her time. A pioneer for women in the genre. Her dedication to precise observation and realistic depiction was remarkable.

Berthe Morisot* (1841-1895)
French. A founder of Impressionist painting who remained at the forefront of the French Impressionist movement. Known for her intimate scenes of everyday life, incorporating elegant colors and delicate brushwork.

* Additional information appears elsewhere in this volume.

Mary Cassatt* (1844-1926)
American expatriated to Paris. Her mother-and-child scenes and genre paintings have been honored only recently in the American art world. Among the best of her generation's Impressionist painters. Her technical skills were superb.

Georgia O'Keeffe* (1887-1986)
American. Perhaps the best-known female painter in America today, and a highly original pioneer in American abstract art. One of the best painters of the twentieth century.

Lyubov Popova* (1889-1924)
Russian. An exceptional painter and an important member of the Russian avant-garde. Her Constructivist style is also highly personal.

Alice Neel (1900-1984)
American. A portrait artist of great intensity and originality. Used her personal insight into the psyches of her subjects to achieve powerful images.

Lois Mailou Jones (1905-   )
African-American. Painter and teacher highly regarded for Cubist-like paintings suggestive of an African influence. Also incorporates other motifs from her travels.

Leonor Fini (1908-   )
Brazilian-born Italian. Associated with Surrealist painters. Her paintings contain Surrealist elements but in a highly individualistic manner.

Frida Kahlo (1910-1954)
Mexican. Disabled painter known for her many self-portraits and a style influenced by Mexican folk painting and Christian symbolism.

Helen Frankenthaler* (1928-   )
American. A major figure in abstract expressionism. Invented the "soak-stain" technique of paint application. Her work evokes the natural world.

"Because of my loneliness and confusion in the social and art worlds, because of my sense that others could not see and respond to the woman Miriam Schapiro as a whole person, I felt increasing pressure alone in my studio. I needed, more than ever, to be a special, different, original artist, to have my art represent me in a clear and unmistakable way, so that I wouldn't have to bother with social identity. My art alone would reveal me to the world and to myself."
Miriam Schapiro*
Quoted in *Working It Out*, 1977

Sculptors and Individualists

The field of sculpture was virtually closed to women until the 1800's. Women have been at the forefront of the contemporary trend toward utilizing unconventional materials like fiber and metals.

Harriet Hosmer* (1830-1908)
American. A major neoclassical sculptor who spent much of her later life in Rome. The most successful female sculptor of the day, especially known for monuments such as *Zenobia*.

Edmonia Lewis* (1845-c. 1911)
Chippewa- and African-American. Sculptor whose early success financed her expatriation to Rome. Her dignified but strongly emotional sculptures reflect her racial and cultural heritage, as well as her identification with women's issues, as in *Hagar in the Wilderness*.

Elisabet Ney* (1833-1907)
German. Sculptor celebrated for her portrait busts, living in Texas in later life. Her former home in Texas now serves as a memorial and museum.

Camille Claudel (1864-1943)
French. Claudel's tragic life and estimable talent were the subject for a recent film. She is remembered for her large-scale allegorical and mythological sculptures and busts as well as for her obsession with her lover and teacher Rodin.

Käthe Kollwitz* (1867-1945)
German. Printmaker and sculptor internationally recognized for powerful images on universal themes such as grief and poverty.

Louise Nevelson* (1899-1988)
Russian-born American. Prominent and much-imitated sculptor, the first to build large-scale environments out of scrap material. Her use of scrap had no historical precedent.

Barbara Hepworth* (1903-1975)
British. Internationally celebrated for her innovative abstract sculpture. Her theme is the relationship between humans and the natural world.

Miriam Schapiro* (1923-   )
Jewish-American. A leader in "pattern painting," her compositions illuminate women's experience. Increasingly popular for her unique and feminist approach to collage, which she calls "femmage." Her work has been reproduced in a popular calendar.

Faith Ringgold (1930-   )
African-American. Combines an interest in African crafts with feminist versions of traditional woman's art. Works in a variety of genres, including murals, soft sculptures(*The Family of Woman* series) and masks.

Magdalena Abakanowicz (1930-   )
Polish. The foremost artist working in fiber today. She has expanded the expressive possibilities of weaving, and more recently has explored fiber and wood sculptures.

Judy Chicago* (1939-   )
American. Best-known for her innovative use of traditional women's crafts in her art, for example in *The Dinner Party*(1979).

American Folk Artists

Although today the distinctions between formal and folk art are blurred, historically artists who worked in certain genres such as quilting were not considered to be true artists. Here are a few artists of the "lesser" genres whose work has been identified and is on display around America. Race or ethnicity indicated where known. Each artist below is represented in several museums, one of which is noted.

Ruth Henshaw Bascom (1771-1848)

Lived in Massachusetts-New Hampshire area.
Known for pastel, crayon, and pencil portraits.
Represented at Abby Aldrich Rockefeller Folk Art Center, Willamsburg, VA.

Michele Felice Corne (1752-1838)

Italian-American. Massachusetts-Rhode Island.
Oil paintings including murals, landscapes and frescoes.
Peabody Museum of Salem, MA.

Ammi Phillips (1788-1865)

Connecticut-Massachusetts.
Oil portraits.
Potsdam Public Museum, Potsdam, NY.

Harriet Powers (1837-1911)

African-American. Georgia.
Quilts.
Smithsonian Institution, Washington, DC.

Jane A. Davis (c.1850)

Massachusetts-Rhode Island.
Watercolor portraits.
Museum of American Folk Art, New York, NY.

Virginia Mason Ivy (c.1850)

Kentucky.
Quilts.
Smithsonian Institution, Washington, DC.

Lucebra Ellis (c. 1850)

Illinois.
Tablecloths.
Illinois State Museum, Springfield, IL.

Anna Mary Robertson Moses* (1860-1961) "Grandma Moses"

American. New York State.
Landscape and memory paintings in oil.
Metropolitan Museum of Art, New York, NY.

Johnston, Effie (1868-1964)
California.
Drawings in pen, ink and colored pensil.
Calaveras County Historical Society, San Andreas, CA.

Clara McDonald Williamson (1875-1976)
Texas.
Memory and genre paintings in oil.
Museum of Modern Art, New York, NY.

Clementine Hunter (b. 1885)
African-American. Louisiana.
Genre and memory paintings in oil
Anglo-American Art Museum, Baton Rouge, LA.

Mattie Lou O'Kelley (1908-)
Georgia.
Farm scenes and memory paintings in oil, acyrlics, and watercolor.
Minneapolis Institute of Arts, Minneapolis, MN.

"I do not want to die until I have faithfully made the most of my talent and cultivated the seed that was placed in me until the last small twig has grown."
Käthe Kollwitz*
Diaries and Letters, 1915

"If I didn't start painting, I would have raised chickens."
Grandma Moses*
My Life's History, 1947

Artworks on View around America

A great deal of work by women artists is on view in American and world museums. The list below is a sampling. Consult the catalog of your local or favorite museum for their holdings. For example, the collection of the Minneapolis Institute of Art includes work by Cassatt, Grace Hartigan, Kollwitz, O'Keeffe, and Vigée-LeBrun, among others. The National Museum of Women in the Arts has the largest American collection of work by women artists, although the collection is judged a conservative one.

Artemisia Gentileschi*
Judith and Maidservant with the Head of Holofernes(c.1625). Oil on canvas.
One of her six versions of the Old Testament story.
Detroit Institute of Arts, Detroit, MI.

Judith Leyster*
Self-Portrait(1635). Oil on canvas.
National Gallery of Art, Washington, DC.

Rosalba Carriera*
Louis XV as a Boy(1720). Pastel on paper.
Museum of Fine Arts, Boston.

Angelica Kauffman*
Cornelia Pointing to Her Children as Her Treasures(1785). Oil on canvas.
Virginia Museum, Richmond, VA.

Adélaïde Labille-Guiard (French, 1747-1803)
Self-Portrait with Two Pupils . . . (1785). Oil on canvas.
Unusual for the artist's inclusion of two outstanding students in order
to introduce them to the public.
Metropolitan Museum of Art, New York, NY.

Lilly Martin Spencer*
The War Spirit at Home(1866). Oil on canvas.
Newark Museum, Newark, NJ.

Rosa Bonheur*
The Horse Fair(1853-5). Oil on canvas.
Perhaps the most famous of Bonheur's work.
Metropolitan Museum of Art, New York, NY.

Berthe Morisot*
Little Girl Reading(1888). Oil on canvas.
Museum of Fine Arts, St. Petersburg, FL.

Mary Cassatt*
The Fitting(1891). Drypoint, softground and aquatint.
Cassatt made ten prints using an unprecedented technique which combined
etching and engraving. An unusual medium for her work.
The Carnegie Museum of Art, Pittsburgh, PA.

Käthe Kollwitz*
The Mothers(1919). Lithograph.
Philadelphia Museum of Art, Philadelphia, PA.

Georgia O'Keeffe*
Red Hills and Bones(1941). Oil on canvas.
Philadelphia Museum of Art, Philadelphia, PA.

Lyubov Popova*
Architectonic Painting(1917). Oil on canvas.
The Museum of Modern Art, New York, NY.

Claire Falkenstein (American, 1908-)
Forum: Memorial to A. Quincy Jones(1987). Orford cedar logs.
An abstract expressionist piece which serves as a metaphor of the cosmos.
California State University, Dominquez Hills, CA.

Louise Nevelson*
Sky Cathedral(1958). Wood, painted black.
Albright-Knox Gallery, Buffalo, NY.

Bettye Saar (African-American, 1926-)
The Liberation of Aunt Jemima(1972). Mixed media.
University Art Museum, Univ. of California at Berkeley, Berkeley, CA.

Helen Frankenthaler*
Flood(1967). Synthetic polymer.
Whitney Museum of American Art, New York, NY.

Elizabeth Murray (American, 1940-)
Sail Baby(1983). Oil on canvas.
A multiple canvas work expressing the tension between personal identity
and emotional bonding with the family.
Walker Art Center, Minneapolis, MN.

*"In a few years it will not be thought strange that women should be preachers and sculptors,
and everyone who comes after us will have to bear fewer and fewer blows.
Therefore I say, I honor all those who step boldly forward, and,
in spite of ridicule and criticism, pave a broader way
for the women of the next generation."*
Harriet Hosmer*

Public Art

Sculpture and other artworks created by women surround us every day in public places around America, in small towns and large. Here are a few examples. A survey of your own town should yield local public pieces by female artists.

ALABAMA
Murals, Post Offices, Tuskegee and Atmore.
>Anne Wilson Goldthwaite(1869-1944)

Stained-glass Window, St. Paul's Episcopal & First Baptist Churches, Selma.
>Clara Weaver Parrish(1861-1952).

CALIFORNIA
Statue, Joan of Arc, San Francisco and replica in San Diego.
>Anna Hyatt Huntington(1876-1973).

CONNECTICUT
Founders Monument, Palisado Green, Palisado Avenue, Windsor.
>Honoring early emigrants.
>Evelyn Beatrice(Batchelder)Longman(1874-1954).

DISTRICT OF COLUMBIA
Bas-relief, *"Agriculture,"* Federal Trade Commission Building, Washington.
>Concetta Scaravaglione(1900-1975).

"Founders of the DAR," DAR Building, Washington.

Memorial for the Titanic, Washington.

"Spirit of the Red Cross," American Red Cross Building, Washington.
>Gertrude Vanderbilt Whitney(1875-1942).

Memorial Sculpture to women of the Upper Louisiana Territory, Jefferson Memorial.
>Nancy Coonsman Hahn(d.1976).

Sculpture, "Forever Free," Howard University.
>Edmonia Lewis*.

Statue, Abraham Lincoln, US Capitol.
>Vinnie Ream Hoxie(1847-1914).

Statue, Frances Willard, Statuary Hall.
>Helen Farnsworth Mears(1872-1916).

Statues, Sam Houston & Stephen S. Austin, Statuary Hall.
>Elisabet Ney*

Vietnam War Memorial, Mall adjacent to Lincoln Memorial.
>Minimalist structure and perhaps the most moving memorial in the US.
>Maya Ying Lin(c. 1960-   ).

IDAHO
State Seal, State Capitol, Boise.
>Depicts a woman a man side by side in support of the state.
>Emma Edwards Green(d. 1942).

ILLINOIS
Figures in the Hall of Man, Field Museum of National History, Chicago.
>Malvina Hoffman(1885-1966).

Statue, *"The Genius of the Telegraph,"* Logan Square, Chicago.
>Evelyn Beatrice(Batchelder) Longman.

Statue, Mother Bickerdyke, Galesburg, Illinois.
>Theo Alice Ruggles Kitson(1871-1932).

INDIANA
Strauss Memorial Fountain, Turkey Run State Park, Rockville.
> Myra Reynolds(n.a.).

IOWA
Statuettes, Kendall Young Library, Webster City.
> Original plaster models of two works.
>> Mary Abastenia St. Leger Eberle(1878-1942).

MASSACHUSETTS
Sculpture, Watertown Public Library, Watertown, Massachusetts.
> Harriet Hosmer*.
Statue, Mary Dyer, State House Grounds, Springfield.
> Honors the Quaker banished for following Anne Hutchinson and later hanged.
>> Sylvia Shaw Judson(1897-1978).
Statue, Samuel Adams, Front of Faneuil Hall, Boston
Statue, Leif Ericsson, Commonwealth Square, Boston
> Anne Whitney(1821-1915).
"Storytime," Framingham Center Library, Framingham, Massachusetts.
> Meta Vaux Warrick(1877-1968).

MICHIGAN
Architectural tiles, St. Paul's Cathedral, Detroit.
> Mary Chase Perry Stratton(1867-1961).

MISSISSIPPI
Statue, Phillis Wheatley, Jackson State University, Jackson.
> Honors the first African-American poet.
>> Elizabeth Catlett(African-American, contemporary).

MISSOURI
Kincaid Fountain, St. Louis Art Museum
> Nancy Coonsman Hahn(d.1976).
Statue, Thomas Hart Benton, Lafayette Park, St. Louis.
> Harriet Hosmer*.

NEBRASKA
Mural, *"The Spirit of Nebraska,"* State Capitol, Lincoln.
> Elizabeth Honor Dolan(1887-1948).

NEW YORK
Bronze sculpture, *"Single Form,"* United Nations Plaza, New York City.
A memorial to Dag Hammarskjold.
> Barbara Hepworth*.
Fountain, *"Angel of the Waters,"* Central Park.
> Hailed as a masterpiece upon its unveiling.
>> Emma Stebbins(1815-1882).
Mural, Slocum Hall, Syracuse University, Syracuse, New York.
> Dedicated to the women of the world.
>> Marion Greenwood(1909-1970).

(New York con't)
Sculpture, top Metropolitan Opera House, Lincoln Center, New York City.
    Mary Callery(1903-1977).
Statue, Kateri Tekakwitha, Shrine of North American Martyrs, Auriesville.
  First Native American candidate for sainthood.
    Adrienne Bouvier(n.a.).

OKLAHOMA
Relief, *"Oklahoma Run,"* Western Heritage Center, Oklahoma City.
    Laura Gardin Fraser(1889-1906).

OREGON
Statue, Sagajawea, Washington Park, Portland.
    Alice Cooper(c. 1910).

PENNSYLVANIA
"Constellation I & II," "Three Birds in Flight," Alcoa Headquarters, Pittsburgh.
    Mary Callery(1903-1977).
Mural, *"The Founding of the State of Liberty Spiritual,"* State Capitol, Harrisburg.
    Violet Oakley(1874-1961).

RHODE ISLAND
Carrie Brown Memorial Fountain, City Hall Park, Providence.
    Enid Yardell(1870-1934).

SOUTH CAROLINA
"Fighting Stallions," Brookgreen Gardens, Murrell's Inlet.
    Anna Hyatt Huntington.

TENNESSEE
Monument to Women of the Confederacy, Nashville and replica in Jackson, MS.
    Belle Kinney Scholz(1890-1959).
Mural, Student Center, University of Tennessee, Knoxville.
  Celebrates Tennessee music from mountain music to jazz.
    Marion Greenwood(1909-1970).

TEXAS
Statues(replicas), Sam Houston, Stephen S. Austin, State Capitol, Austin
    Elisabet Ney*.

UTAH
Mural, *"Western Town,"* Helper Post Office, Helper.
    Jenne Magafan(1916-1952).

VIRGINIA
"The Hiker," **Veterans' Memorial,** Arlington Cemetery, Arlington.
    Theo Alice Ruggles Kitson(1871-1932).

WISCONSIN
Statue, *"The Genius of Wisconsin,"* State Capitol, Madison.
    Helen Farnsworth Mears(1872-1916).

14

Builders and Designers

Architecture remains an unusual field for women. Some countries are more encouraging than others: in Scandinavian countries, women make up about 20% of all architects. In the United States and many other nations, the percentage is only 5.

Melusina Fay Peirce (c.1850)
American. Proponent of co-operative housekeeping associations and the holder of a patent for a co-operative apartment house design.

Alice Constance Austin (c. 1900)
American. Designer of a kitchenless house. Also the architect of the co-operative colony at Llano del Rio, California. Supported the notion of feminist socialist cities.

Julia Morgan (1872-1957)
American. Most prolific of the early female architects, designing nearly 1000 buildings including San Simeon, the Hearst estate. She served as mentor for many women on her staff.

Sophia Hayden (c.1868-1953)
Hispanic-American. Remembered for her award-winning design of the celebrated Woman's Building at the World's Columbian Exposition in Chicago, 1893.

Louise Blanchard Bethune (1856-1913)
American. Best-known female architect of the late 19th century. Designed many schools and stores in Western New York State.

Marion Mahony Griffin (1871-1961)
American. Artist-architect associated with Frank Lloyd Wright and the avant-garde movement of the turn-of-the-century. Known for her imaginative style.

Sibyl Moholy-Nagy (1903-1971)
German-American. Architectural critic, historian, and teacher. A critic of functionalist design, she defended the expressiveness of architecture in form and content.

Jane Jacobs* (1916-   )
American, now living in Canada. Her book *The Life and Death of American Cities*(1961) singlehandedly redirected city planning thinking toward smaller-scale buildings and neighbor-hoods. Influential critic and advocate.

Ada Louise Huxtable (1921-   )
American. Longtime architectural critic and editor of the *New York Times*. An important figure in educating the public to appreciate the buildings surrounding them.

Luz Amorocho (early 20th century)
Colombian. Esteemed teacher and architect of many institutional spaces. Considered the "grand old woman" of the field in Colombia and a role model for many young professionals.

Gae Aulenti (c.1931-   )
Italian. Eclectic architect working in interior and product design as well as conventional fields. A key figure in the well-known design network in Milan.

Denise Scott Brown (1931-)
Zimbabwe-born Briton. Social advocate in the field of urban design and planning, particularly in the Philadelphia area. Her concern is balancing social and aesthetic needs.

Birgit Cold (n.a.)
Norwegian. Teacher and architect especially involved with social housing. She believes that housing design should be inclusive, reflecting the aspirations of all members of society.

Itsuko Hasegawa* (1941-)
Japanese. Internationally-recognized for her designs of public and private spaces including the Shonandai Cultural Centre.

Louise St. John Kennedy (1950-)
Australian. Award-winning architect and designer of domestic spaces, working on her country's west coast.

Elizabeth Plater-Zyberk (1950-)
American. A major contributor to 1980s architecture in Florida in both town and private home design. She promotes compact communities as an alternative to suburban sprawl.

"For several years my practice has been based on the concept of architecture as an interpretation of nature, instead of thinking of it as something totally based on reason and rationality . . .
In Japan, the light, the wind, and even the air changes with the seasons,
and it has been my objective to create spaces that enable one to co-exist with nature."
Itsuko Hasegawa*

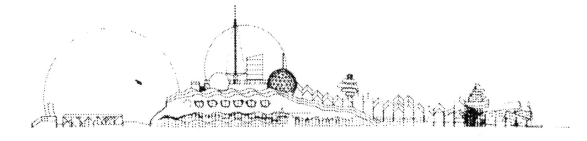

History

" *The dogma of woman's complete historical subjection to man must be rated as one of the most fantastic myths ever created by the human mind.* "
Mary Ritter Beard
Woman as A Force in History, 1946

" *My great-grandmama told my grandmama the part she lived through that my grandmama didn't live through and my grandmama told my mama what they both lived through and my mama told me what they all lived through and we were supposed to pass it down like that from generation to generation so we'd never forget.* "
Gayl Jones
Corregidora, 1975

Prominent Dates in American History

Social history is more descriptive of the lives of women than the name and date-oriented political history we are taught in school. The outline below attempts to wed the two.

1636 Anne Hutchinson banished from Massachusetts Bay Colony as a religious heretic and non-conforming woman.

1692 Height of the witchhunts in Salem, MA. Fourteen women and six men are executed for witchcraft. Hundreds are accused and imprisoned, mostly women.

1776 Abigail Adams writes to husband John to request that the Continental Congress "remember the ladies." John Adams' correspondence later indicates he considered the idea of granting women more rights within the Declaration of Independence but believed that doing so would open the door to other "dependent" groups.

1820's Young women enter the new textile mills of New England to work. They are mostly white women from surrounding farms and they are boarded in dormitory-like settings.

1828 First strike by women workers, by the cotton mill workers in Dover, NH.

1832 First female anti-slavery society founded by black women in Salem, MA.
It is the first of many similar societies.

1834 Oberlin College founded near Cleveland, OH. It is the first and only college to admit women and African-Americans.

1848 July 19 & 20. First Women's Rights Convention* held at Seneca Falls, NY.

1849 Research by a British professor offers physicians the first accurate information about the female fertility cycle. The research is published in the US in the 1850s.

1850's Harriet Tubman "steals" some 300 slaves from the South via the Underground Railroad. A $40,000 reward stands for the capture of "Moses," dead or alive.

1860 First Homestead Act(second in 1890) allows both women and men to homestead free land. For the first time, a wife or single woman could control the title to a piece of land.

1863 Emancipation Proclamation frees slaves, but the subsequent 15th Amendment only grants black men the right to vote.

1869 National Woman Suffrage Organization founded by Stanton* and Anthony*. One year later, the American Woman Suffrage Organization founded by a competing group of feminists.

1889 Jane Addams* founds Hull House*.

1896 National Council of Jewish Women founded.

1896 National Association of Colored Women founded.

1900 Five million female wage earners contribute to the American economy. Those most likely to be working outside the home are black women , immigrant women, and single women.

1904 Mary McCleod Bethune* founds her first school in Florida.

1909 *Uprising of the 20,000.* Waistmakers and dressmakers strike New York City factories for better working conditions and the International Ladies' Garment Workers' Union is transformed from a miniscule group to a powerful union of thousands.

1910 Triangle Shirtwaist Factory fire kills 146, mostly women and children.

1912 Henrietta Szold founds Hadassah.

1916 Alice Paul* establishes the Natinal Woman's Party(NWP).

1917 January. Women from the NWP begin picketing the White House. In the summer, arrests would begin. The women refused bail, were imprisoned and some were force-fed.

1917 World War I begins and thousands of women replace male workers who go off to war.

1917 Margaret Sanger* opens her first birth control clinic. It is quickly shut down. By 1932, more than 80 clinics would be in operation.

1920 August 26. Women are allowed to vote with the ratification of the19th Amendment*. Shortly thereafter, a cultural backlash speeds the first wave of feminists into near invisibility.

1921 First beauty pageant held in Atlantic City.

1922 Judith Kaplan Eisenstein celebrates the first Bat Mitzvah ever. It is sung by her father, Rabbi Mordecai Kaplan.

1923 Equal Rights Amendment(ERA)* first introduced into Congress.

1925 Nellie Taylor Ross becomes the first female governor in the US.

1932 Chinese Women's Association founded in New York City.

1933 Frances Perkins* becomes the first female Cabinet member in American history.

1941 America enters the Second World War and millions of women replace male workers. Many women remained in the work force after the War, despite popular opinion encouraging their return to the home.

1960 The first birth control pill is approved for public use. The FDA later discovers that approval was based on research using only 130 women.

1961 Kennedy appoints a Presidential Commission on the Status of Women which will complete the first comprehensive investigation of the status of American women.

1963 *The Feminine Mystique* * is published and widely discussed.

1964 Senator Margaret Chase Smith is nominated for President at the Republican convention.

1965 Casey Hayden and Mary King circulate a memo among women involved in the civil rights struggle. The document calls for a separate women's movement.

1966 National Organization of Women founded.

1968 Chicago Women's Liberation Movement publishes the first newsletter of the emerging women's movement. Hundreds of newsletters, journals, and newspapers would appear.

1969 Boston Women's Health Book Collective publishes *Our Bodies, Ourselves.* The landmark feminist health book sells 250,000 its first year and goes on to sell millions more.

1970 August 26. Thousands of women strike around America to commemorate the 50th anniversary of suffrage and to protest the continued discrimination of women.

1972 Shirley Chisholm* runs for President, the first African-American and first woman to campaign for the nomination of a major political party.

1973 National Black Feminist Organization founded.

1975 International Year of the Woman declared by the United Nations.

1984 Geraldine A. Ferraro becomes the first female vice-presidential candidate of a major political party.

1990 Nearly fifty-seven million women wage earners now boast the American economy. Forty-five percent of the total labor force is female.

1992 Susan Faludi's book, *Backlash:The Undeclared War on American Women* is a runaway best-seller. It is the first thorough-going investigation attempts to eliminate the gains of the second wave of the American women's movement.

"Like their personal lives, women's history is fragmented, interrupted; a shadow history of human beings whose existence has been shaped by the efforts and demands of others."
Elizabeth Janeway
Women:Their Changing Roles, 1973

Political Leaders & Heads of State

Until recently, women achieved high office through marriage or family connections. They often were forced to use indirect means to secure real power. As the list below suggests, the indirect methods could be brutal.

Hatshepsut (1503-1482 BC)

Egyptian. Powerful influence on her half-brother/husband. After his death, she became Regent and then Pharaoh—the first woman to hold the position in 2000 years. Her reign is associated with prosperity and vibrant cultural life. A mortuary temple in her honor still stands in Thebes.

Theodora (497-548 AD)

Byzantine. A learned orphan who married the heir to the throne and assumed many of his duties. Reported to be merciless to opponents. She is unique for her passionate advocacy of justice and a higher status for women.

Wu Chao (625-705)

China. She began as a concubine and usurped the throne after eliminating those in her way. Enjoyed a half-century of power, establishing peace and prosperity, a flourishing culture, and the unification of China. Indomitable until the end, she retired at age 80.

Eleanor of Aquitaine (1122-1202)

French, living part of her life in Britain. One of the most powerful women of her day. Duchess of Aquitaine, a French province, and Queen of France and England at different times. Influential both politically and culturally. She gathered the finest poets, musicians, and other artists at her court. Engaged in complicated political intrigues involving husband Henry II and her sons. Memorialized in the play and film *The Lion in Winter* (1966, 1968).

Catharine the Great (1729-1796)

German-Russian. Deposed her husband, declared herself head of state and assumed total authority. St. Petersburg became a center of culture during her time and Russian grew into a leading power in Europe. Corresponded with Voltaire and other Enlightenment figures, initiated some progressive reforms but stifled dissent.

Elizabeth I (1533-1603) *"The Virgin Queen"*

British. This well-educated monarch's long reign and charismatic image encouraged a flourishing culture; Shakespeare wrote during her time. Also England became a secure and a commercial power on her watch. Her character has fascinated scholars and artists for centuries; she is the subject of many books, treatises, plays, and films.

Nancy (Langhorne) Astor (1879-1964)

American-British. First female member of Parliament, at first elected to replace her second husband when he was promoted. She served from 1919 to 1945 and is remembered for her unusual combination of flamboyance and an intolerant moral stance. A PBS series several years ago chronicled her life and times.

Frances Perkins* (1882-1965)

American. An activist on working women's rights and conditions, she was appointed to government in New York State and grew friendly with FDR and Eleanor Roosevelt. She became the first woman in any Cabinet post when FDR named her Secretary of Labor. She drafted the landmark Social Security Act(1935), the National Labor Relations Act(1935), and the Wages and Hours Act(1938). The building housing the present Department of Labor is named in her honor.

Dolores Ibarruri (1895-   ) *"La Pasionaria"*

Spanish. Her working-class heritage led her into the early Spanish Communist Party; she was elected to Parliament in 1936. Considered a brilliant orator and the most inspiring of Loyalist (anti-Franco)leaders. She helped establish the Popular Front government to counter Franco's dictatorship. After his death, she returned to Spain from exile and was re-elected to Parliament at the age of 81.

Golda Meir(Meyerson) (1898-1978)

Ukrainian-born American-Israeli. Emigrated to Palestine with her husband and became involved with the Palestine labor movement and then with the Zionists. She assumed many positions in the new Israeli government, including UN delegate from 1953 to 1966 and eventually became Prime Minister, serving from 1969 to 1974. Remembered for both toughness and warmth.

Indira Gandhi (1917-1984)

Indian. Served as host and key supporter for her father Nehru from 1947 to 1964 and replaced her father in the Indian Parliament at his death. Made Prime Minister in 1966, serving until 1977 and then again from 1980 until 1984, when she was assassinated. Considered ruthless and autocratic but praised for loosening the USSR grip on India and speaking out forcefully on the rights of poorer nations.

Evita(Eva) Perón (1919-1952)

Argentinian. Stage and screen star who married political comer Juan Perón and supported his presidential bid with her charismatic speeches and presence. Her candidacy for vice-president in Perón's second term was later withdrawn. Shortly thereafter, her health deteriorated rapidly. Her powerful persona was resurrected in the musical *Evita*(1979).

Shirley Chisholm* (1924-   )

African-American. New York State and later US Representative who ran for the Presidency in 1972. An outspoken and eloquent advocate for the rights of women and minority peoples. The title of her autobiography expresses her ethical convictions: *Unbought and Unbossed*(1970).

Margaret Thatcher (1925-   ) *"The Iron Lady"*

British. Daughter of a grocer who became a lawyer then member of Parliament in 1959. She assumed the role of Conservative Prime Minister twenty years later. Reputedly intransigent with others in her Cabinet on both economic policies and political decisions. She was forced out in 1991 but continues to speak out on political and economic issues.

Vigdis Finnbogadottir (1930-)

Icelander. President of Iceland since 1980. Theatrical producer and educator who entered politics with a left-wing agenda and later became the first democratically-elected female head of state.

Patricia Schroeder (1940-)

American. As a long-time US representative, she is a strong advocate for women's and family issues. Candidate for the Presidency in 1988. An acknowledged expert on defense issues as a result of her active participation on the Armed Services Committee.

*"We Americans have the chance to become someday a nation in which all racial stocks
and classes can exist in their own selfhoods, but meet on a basis of respect and equality
and live together, socially, economically, and politically. We can become a dynamic equilibrium,
a harmony of many different elements, in which the whole will be greater than all its parts
and greater than any society the world has seen before. It can still happen."*
Shirley Chisholm*
The Good Fight, 1973

*"Once in a Cabinet we had to deal with the fact that there had been an outbreak
of assaults on women at night. One minister suggested a curfew:
women should stay home after dark. I said, 'But it's the men
who are attacking the women. If there's to be a curfew,
let the men stay home, not the women."*
Golda Meir*

"I keep my campaign promises, but I never promised to wear stockings."
Ella Grasso
former governor of Connecticut

"Women are not more moral, we are only uncorrupted by power."
Gloria Steinem*
Speech, 1970

*"I am not elevating women to sainthood, nor am I suggesting that all women
share the same views, or that all women are good and all men bad.
Women have screamed for war. Women, like men, have stoned black children
going to integrated schools. Women have been and are prejudiced, narrow-minded,
reactionary, even violent. Some women. They, of course, have a right to vote and
a right to run for office. I will defend that right, but I will not support them or vote for them."*
Bella Abzug
Speech, 1971

Milestones in American Legal History

Under British law, women held no separate legal status, unless they were independent, widowed or held property. America adopted the same principles of law.

1776 Declaration of Independence
A strenuously-argued statement opposing slavery is excluded from the final draft. Women are not mentioned, but the document states that all men are created equal.

1787 Constitution
The Constitution excludes women and many men from full citizenship.

1819 Dartmouth College v. Woodward
The Supreme Court rules on a contract law dispute and draws a comparison to the civil contract of marriage: *"A man has as good a right to his wife, as to the property acquired under a marriage contract . . . He has a legal right to her society and her fortune . . . "*

1830-1900 Married Women's Property Acts
Many states, especially in the Northeast and Midwest, pass measures which raise the legal status of women with regard to the writing of wills, control over wages, separate estates, widows' access to husband's estate and other issues pertinent to the middle-class. Some legislative gains occur in child custody and divorce law; children are increasingly awarded to the mother.

1848 Declaration of Sentiments
The document prepared by the first Women's Rights Convention at Seneca Falls offers an alternative to the Declaration of Independence. The document challenges the subordination of women within the family.

1867 Fifteenth Amendment
Women's advocates fail to convince Congress to include women in the 15th Amendment, which extends suffrage(the right to vote) to black men. Some advocates resort to racist tactics in the struggle.

1873 Bradwell v. Illinois
The Supreme Court denies Myra Bradwell, a married woman, the right to practice law, stating that this right is not a privilege of citizenship and is not a privilege extended to women.

1875 Minor v. Happersett
Virginia Minor attempted to vote, but was refused registration. The Supreme Court holds that women are not included in suffrage extended by the Constitution although they are citizens and persons. The decision ends suffragists' endeavors to claim that women have the vote because they are citizens.

1894 Re Lockwood
The Supreme Court allows states to confine their definition of "person" to the male gender.

1896 Plessy v. Ferguson
The Supreme Court holds that separate-but-equal facilities are constitutional. The decision allows segregationist practices in the South until it is overruled in 1954.

1908 Muller v. Oregon

The Supreme Court states that limitations can be placed on women's working hours and conditions, because of their ability to bear children. The decision initiates an era of legislation protecting women from excessive hours and debilitating work conditions. "Protective legislation" is argued hotly among women's groups. Some believe that such legislation is a necessary benefit for working women although it involves sexism; other groups believe that the benefits of protection do not outweigh the degree to which they undermine equal rights.

1920 19th Amendment

The Amendment grants adult women the right to vote and ends a suffrage campaign of 72 years.

1923 Equal Rights Amendment

After discussion and drafting by several feminist groups, Alice Paul finalizes the wording of the ERA and the National Woman's Party and other groups lobby for the Amendment's introduction into Congress.

1923 Adkins v. Children's Hospital

The Supreme Court holds that minimum wages for women are unconstitutional, since special protection is no longer needed because women now may vote.

1924 Radice v. New York

The Court restricts the right of women to work at night.

1937 West Coast Hotel v. Parrish

The Supreme Court reverses Adkins and grants minimum wage rights to women and minors.

1963 Equal Pay Act

Congress prohibits wage discrimination among workers performing the same job for reasons of race, color, religion, sex, or national origin.

1964 Title VII of the Civil Rights Act

Congress prohibits discrimination in employment based on race, creed, national origin, or sex. This legislation created the Equal Employment Opportunities Commission(EEOC).

1972 Title IX of the Educational Amendments Act

Congress prohibits sex discrimination in all public undergraduate institutions and in most institutions receiving any federal monies.

1972 ERA Progress

After 49 years, Congress passes the ERA and it is sent to the states for ratification.

1973 Roe v. Wade

The Supreme Court upholds a woman's right to abortion, based on the right of privacy between a woman and her doctor. The decision is the first to legalize abortion since many states criminalized the practice in the late 1800s.

1984 Roberts et al v. US Jaycees

The Supreme Court holds that accepting women as members does not abridge the male freedom of association.

1986 Meritor Savings Bank v. Vinson

The Court rules that sexual harassment of an employee by a supervisor violates laws against sex discrimination. The decision opens the door on legal remedies for sexual harassment.

1989 Webster v. Reproductive Health Services

The Supreme Court reconsiders Roe v. Wade and recognizes the states' compelling interest in life from conception. The decision encourages restrictive legislation on abortion at the state level.

1991 International Union et al. v. Johnson Controls, Inc.

The Supreme Court holds that women cannot be excluded from jobs involving exposure to hazardous chemicals because of their reproductive function. Sex is not considered a *bona fide* job requirement in such work.

"As when the slaves who got their freedom had to take it over or under or through the unjust forms of the law, precisely so now must women take it to get their right to a voice in this government."
Susan B. Anthony*
Speech, 1873

*You may wear your silks and satin,
Go when and where you please,
Make embroidery and tattin',
And live quite at your ease.
You may go to ball and concert,
In gaudy hat and coat,
In fact, my charming creatures,
Do everything but VOTE.*
From *"Female Suffrage"*
Words by R. A. Cohen(mid-1800s)

"Indulgence is given women as a substitute for justice."
Harriet Martineau
Society in America, 1837

Suffrage Around the World

In countries formerly held as colonies, white women typically were enfranchised before black women or men. The date of universal suffrage--for all men and all women--is given below.

New Zealand	1893	Yugoslavia	1945
Finland	1906	China	1949
Norway	1913	El Salvador	1950
Poland	1919	Greece	1952
West Germany	1919	Mexico	1953
United States	1920	Pakistan	1956
United Kingdom	1928	Canada	1960
Brazil	1932	Kenya (at independence)	1963
Turkey	1934	Kuwait (all women and most men still waiting)	
France	1944		
Vietnam	1945		

Oh, all the men make all the laws,
which makes the women fret,
But wait and see those laws
when we at last our suffrage get.

'Yes, Papa votes, but Mama can't,
Oh, no, not yet, not yet.
And I'll not marry any man,
till I my suffrage get.'
From *"I am a Suffragette"*
Words by M. Olive Drennen(early 1900's)

"No change in society has even been seen or envisioned as deeply as the prospect of equality of the sexes. None of the great revolutions has altered the most fundamental relationship of all, that between man and woman--not the abolition of classes envisioned by the great political and economic revolutionaries; not the spread of the great religions of the world; not the eradication of racial prejudice, for which we still toil. To alter the economic and political order, to be sure, is to change society very profoundly indeed. To raise the blight of racial bigotry is to rediscover the principles of both humanism and Judeo-Christian ethics. But basic as would be the changes, they would change society, not civilization, as sexual equality would. For the inequality of the sexes is the oldest inequality of all, preceding both class and racial discrimination and tapping us at our most vulnerable sources."

Eleanor Holmes Norton*
Speech, 1970

No golden weights can turn the scale
Of justice in His sight;
And what is wrong in woman's life
In man's cannot be right.
Frances E. W. Harper*
"A Double Standard", late 1800's

"I never doubted that equal rights was the right direction.
Most reforms, most problems are complicated.
But to me there is nothing complicated about ordinary equality."
Alice Paul*
Interview, *American Heritage 1972*

She walketh veiled and sleeping,
For she knoweth not her power;
She obeyeth but the pleading
Of her heart, and the high leading
Of her soul, unto this hour.
Slow advancing, halting, creeping,
Comes the Woman to the hour!--
She walketh veiled and sleeping,
For she knoweth not her power.
Charlotte Perkins Gilman*
"She Walketh Veiled and Sleeping," early 1900's

Activists

Jeanne D'Arc (1412?-1431) *"Maid of Orlèans"*
French. Visions led her toward freeing France from England's grip and the coronation of the true king. She accomplished all that at the head of an army, was captured eventually, convicted and burned at the stake as a heretic. She was canonized in the 20th century and a moving memorial stands at the scene of her death in Rouen.

Sojourner Truth (Isabella van Wagener) (1777-1883)
African-American. Born in slavery. As a free woman, visions commanded her to take a new name and speak out against slavery. As Sojourner Truth, she began speaking before abolitionist and later women's rights groups—an extremely unusual, even dangerous, role for a black woman at that time. A powerful, charismatic orator.

Elizabeth Cady Stanton* (1815-1902)
American. The leading light of the 19th-century women's movement. Co-organizer of the first women's rights convention at Seneca Falls in 1848. Her views were quite radical for the time and she became a persuasive writer, as in *The Woman's Bible*(1895-98), and a dynamic speaker.

Susan B. Anthony* (1820-1906)
American. With Stanton, indomitable leader of the 19th-century women's movement. Involved with temperance and abolition issues prior to her feminist work. Founded national and international suffrage organizations. Edited the journal, *The Revolution*. With Stanton and Matilda Gage, authored the monumental *History of Woman Suffrage*(1886).

Louise Michel (1830-1895)
French. Socialist, revolutionary, and tireless campaigner on social and educational issues. Known for her impassioned oratory. Imprisoned for 17 years at different times for her views.

Mary (Harris) Jones* (1830-1930) *"Mother Jones"*
Irish-born American. Labor leader who, as a widow, became an organizer for the United Mine Workers. She opposed the women's suffrage movement, believing it a diversion from the class struggle. Heavily involved in the mining strikes of the 1910s.

Emmeline Pankhurst (1858-1928)
British. Formed the suffrage-oriented Women's Social and Political Union in 1903 and increasingly adopted what were then militant tactics. Considered a brilliant orator and autocratic administrator. Arrested many times campaigning for suffrage, but when World War I erupted, directed her efforts toward the war. Although she never reinvolved herself in the final years before suffrage was granted, Mrs. Pankhurst was the most significant advocate for British women's suffrage. Daughter Christabel(1880-1958) worked alongside her mother and later turned to evangelism. Daughter Sylvia(Estelle)(1882-1960) broke early on with Emmeline and Christabel and worked, especially through her art, on bringing working and middle-class reform movements together. The story of "The Fighting Pankhursts" is told in *Shoulder to Shoulder*(1975), which itself was adapted into a public television series.

Jane Addams* (1860-1935)
American. As a young social worker, she founded Hull House* and came to exert substantial influence on local and national legislation, especially on the treatment of juvenile urban crime. An active suffragist and pacifist(winner of the Nobel Peace Prize), and a founding member of the American Civil Liberties Union(ACLU) in 1920.

Ida B. Wells-(Barnet) (1862-1931)
African-American. Journalist, newspaper owner, anti-lynching crusader, and later suffragist.
A co-founder of the NAACP, although her views were more militant, and founder of the first black women's suffrage organization. Chiefly remembered for her long campaign against the horrors of lynching in the Southern States

Alexandra Kollontai (1871-1952)
Russian. Revolutionary, feminist, pacifist and politician whose reputation and writings gain renewed visibility in the 1970s. An ardent opponent of World War I. Served in the first Bolshevik government and campaigned for reforms in domestic life. Later fell out of favor and was assigned as ambassador to Finland. There she was a key figure in the peace negotiations ending the Soviet-Finnish war of 1944.

Rosa Luxemburg (1870-1919) *"Red Rosa"*
Jewish-Polish-German. Socialist, feminist, and pacifist, a founder of the German Communist Party. Energetic organizer and writer focused on the achievement of worker solidarity.
She was shot by her political opponents.

Mary McCleod Bethune* (1875-1955)
African-American. Her parents were born as slaves and she became one of the most powerful women in America. Founded a school in Florida, now Bethune-Cookman College*, and later established the National Council of Negro Women(NCNW). In Washington, she came to know Eleanor Roosevelt and was a trusted advisor. Appointed by FDR to be Director of Negro Affairs in the National Youth Administration.

Margaret Sanger* (1883-1966)
American. In 1920, opened the first birth control clinic in Brooklyn and was arrested for her trouble. Because of her leadership in the fight for legal birth control, more than 80 clinics operated in America by 1932. She believed birth control to be an attack on poverty and used her considerable influence in the 1950s to promote the development of the Pill.

Alice Paul* (1885-1977)
American. While working in England on a graduate thesis, Paul met the Pankhursts and involved herself in their struggle. Returning home, she founded the National Woman's Party and utilized similarly militant tactics to advocate for the vote(*Jailed for Freedom*, 1920). She later drafted the ERA and lobbied for its passage until her death.

Gloria Steinem (1934-)
American. A leading feminist and co-founder of *Ms.* magazine in 1972. Best-selling author(*Everyday Acts and Outrageous Rebellions*, 1983). Successful free-lance journalist for many years before and after her involvement with the women's movement.

Eleanor Holmes Norton* (1937-)
African-American. Long time professor at Georgetown Law School and a leader on both civil rights and feminist causes. Eloquent writer and speaker who now represents the District of Columbia in Congress.

Eleanor Smeal (1939-)
American. An early president of the National Organization for Women(NOW) and founder of the Fund for the Feminist Majority. An inspiring speaker and tireless campaigner for women's rights.

*"We are in for a very, very long haul . . . I am asking for everything you have to give.
We will never give up . . . You will lose your youth, your sleep, your patience,
your sense of humor and occasionally, the understanding and support of people
who love you very much. In return, I have nothing to offer you but your pride
in being a woman, and all the dreams you've ever had for your daughters
and nieces and granddaughters . . . your future and the certain knowledge
that at the end of your days you will be able to look back and say
that once in your life you gave everything you had for justice."*
Jill Ruckelshaus
Speech, 1977

*"Reformers must expect to be disowned by those
who are only too happy to enjoy
what has been won for them."*
Doris Lessing
The Golden Notebook, 1962

"We specialize in the wholly impossible."
Nannie Helen Burroughs*
Motto, Burroughs Training School, Washington

Halls of Fame

Halls of fame honor significant women in history ar in contemporary life. Some are efforts sanctioned by state organizations; others are private efforts. Here is a partial listing.

National Women's Hall of Fame

76 Fall Street, Seneca Falls, NY.
Established in 1973 at the site of the 1848 Women's Rights Convention*.
Operated by a non-profit corporation.
(*see* Women's Rights National Historical Park under *Landmarks*)

National Cowgirl Hall of Fame

515 Avenue B, Hereford, TX.
Established 1975.
Honors women who have contributed significantly to our Western heritage as cowgirls, pioneers, professionals, or in other ways. Inductees include Sacajawea*, Laura Ingalls Wilder, suffragist and sculptor Lilla Day Monroe.

Alabama Women's Hall of Fame

Marion.
Established in 1970 at Judson College.

Hall of Fame of Delaware Women

Wilmington.
Established in 1981 by the Delaware Commission on the Status of Women.

Iowa Women's Hall of Fame

507-10th Street, Des Moines.
Established in 1975 by the Iowa Commission on the Status of Women.

Michigan Women's Hall of Fame

213 West Main Street, Lansing.
Established in 1987 by the Michigan Women's Studies Association.
Developed an "Historic Women of Michigan Theme Trail" (map available).

" A journey without history is like a portrait of an old face without its wrinkles."
Freya Madeline Stark*, *The Lycian Shore*, 1956

Women's Heritage Trails & Museums

Museums, trails and tours highlight landmarks, events and eras as well as outstanding women. Most efforts listed below were launched by individuals or private organizations.

UNITED STATES
Women's-History-Museum-on-the-Road
JR Enterprises, Box 209, West Liberty, WV.
Bus exhibits and personal collection of Jeanne Schramm.

CALIFORNIA
Women's Heritage Museum
1509 Portola, Palo Alto, CA .
Brainchild of director Jeanne Farr McDonnell. Operates as a museum without walls, lending out a California suffrage exhibit and several displays.

DISTRICT OF COLUMBIA
Feminist Walking Tour of Capitol Hill
PO Box 30563, Bethesda MD.
Designed by The Feminist Institute and available through group tour or by self-guided pamphlet.

LOUISIANA
Women's History Walking Tour of New Orleans
421 Manasses Place, New Orleans.
The book *Women and New Orleans—A History* includes a walking tour; the author conducts tours of the city.

MASSACHUSETTS
Boston Women's Heritage Trail
c/o Dr. Patricia C. Morris, 75 New Dudley Street, Boston.
Researched and prepared by schoolchildren and inaugurated in 1990. Booklet and information available.

MICHIGAN
Women's Heritage Trail
c/o Michigan Women's Hall of Fame, 213 W. Main St. in Lansing.
An *"Historic Women of Michigan Theme Trail"* map is available.

MINNESOTA
Women's History Tour of the Twin Cities
This book, written in1982 by Karen Mason and Carol Lacey, may be found in libraries or used book stores in the area. The tour notes landmarks in the Minneapolis-St. Paul area.

OHIO
Women's History Trail
c/o Akron Area Women's History Project,PO Box 80158, Akron.
Women of Summit County: A Self-Guided Tour includes a text and audio tape.

Historic Landmarks Associated with Women

Hundreds of local, state and national landmarks of special interest to women have been restored and preserved for posterity.
All the buildings below are historically significant and many are architecturally significant.
A few are private dwellings.

ALABAMA
Ivy Green, Tuscumbia.
Helen Keller(1880-1968) was born at Ivy Green. It was here that teacher Anne Sullivan Macy(1866-1936) first taught Helen Keller, those experiences later immortalized in the drama *The Miracle Worker*(1957). Helen Keller became an author and deaf-blind worker for the blind.

ALASKA
Alaska Nellie's Homestead, Lawing.
Nellie Neal Lawing(1874-1956) began as a cook for railroad crews and later turned hunter and trapper, dog-musher, miner and post office manager. She also found time to lecture on the area's wildlife. Her roadhouse is now a natural history museum which includes artifacts from the early days of Alaska as well as Lawings' letters.

DISTRICT OF COLUMBIA
Nannie Helen Burroughs* School, Grant Street.
Burroughs(1878-1961) had great difficulty finding a teaching or clerking position in Washington because of her color. She later founded the School to train black women in "respectable" careers and for expert homemaking. The Burroughs Schools has trained thousands from America and other countries and is now an elementary school.

Sewall-Belmont House, Constitution Avenue.
Alva Erskine Smith Vanderbilt Belmont(1853-1933) was the benefactor of Alice Paul's* National Woman's Party and provided the funds to purchase this house for the NWP in 1921. It remains the organization's headquarters. Alice Paul lived in the house with other members during the final years of the suffrage campaign. Busts of Belmont, Paul and other suffrage leaders are on display. The Belmont house is now maintained by the National Park Service.

FLORIDA
Bethune-Cookman College/Mary M. Bethune House,Daytona Beach.
Bethune-Cookman College is the latest incarnation of the school Mary McCleod Bethune* founded in 1904. She retired to the house in Daytona Beach in 1949 after many decades as an influential leader and government official in Washington.

Marjorie Kinnan Rawlings* House Museum, Cross Creek.
The restored Rawlings home reflects the time when Marjorie Kinnan Rawlings wrote about the surrounding area in her Pulitzer Prize-winning *The Yearling*(1938) and in the memoir(and 1983 film), *Cross Creek*(1942).

GEORGIA
The Hambidge Center, Rabun Gap.
Mary Crovatt Hambidge(1885-1973) revived traditional mountain weaving in her native state and established this center as a place for the weavers to manufacture and market their products. It now serves as a retreat for artists, writers, and other creative people. Products from the original Center are on exhibit at the Smithsonian, the Museum of Modern Art and museums abroad.

ILLINOIS
Hull House*, Chicago.
Jane Addams* and her companion Ellen Gates Starr rented part of the Hull mansion in 1889 so they might work with the poor. At the time, the house was surrounded by neighborhoods of European immigrants. Addams lived here the rest of her life and Hull House became a complex of buildings. Hull House is restored to its original condition and serves as a museum.

INDIANA
The Madame C. J. Walker Manufacturing Company, Indianapolis.
Sarah Breedlove Walker(1867-1919) became the first black female millionaire. A sharecropper's daughter, she devised methods for straightening hair and eventually employed 3000 workers to make and sell her products. The Company is renovated for use as a cultural space.

LOUISIANA
Melrose Plantation House, Melrose.
Marie Therèse(Coincoin) Metoyer(1742?-1816?) was given freedom from slavery by her lover. He gave her land for a home, now known as Maison de Marie Therèse and located near Bermuda. The Maison is a hip-roofed Creole cottage. As a successful businesswoman and proud African, Marie Metoyer purchased Melrose land and built, with her children,the Melrose Plantation. Its buildings are thought to be the oldest of African design in America built by black Americans for black Americans.

MASSACHUSETTS
Sargent-Murray-Gilman-Hough House, Gloucester.
Judith Sargent Stevens Murray(1751-1820) is remembered for her staunch advocacy of women's rights in late 1700's essays well before the women's movement began in America. She lived here as a child and then with two successive husbands.

Hancock Shaker Village, Hancock.
Ann Lee(1736-1784) is credited with introducing the Shaker religion to the Colonies upon her arrival in 1774. Several of the 11 settlements established still exist around the US. Hancock was founded in the 1780's, during Lee's lifetime. The village includes 20 structures on 1000 acres. More than 300 Shakers lived here at one time.

Mitchell House, Nantucket Island.
Astronomer Maria Mitchell* discovered "her" comet here in her childhood home. The home now serves as a library, museum, and aquarium.

NEW JERSEY
Paulsdale, Mount Laurel.
ERA author and suffragist Alice Paul* grew up in this frame house. It is among the most recently-named National Historic Landmarks associated with women. The Alice Paul Foundation is attempting to purchase the home for use as a leadership center for women and girls.

NEW YORK
Henry Street Settlement, New York City.
Lillian Wald(1867-1940) was a nurse with concern about living conditions on the East Side. She founded the Settlement as a volunteer nursing service in 1893; it grew into a complex of social and cultural institutions and was acknowledged as a great urban center of social service. Public health nurses lived here and hosted the luminaries of the settlement movement such as Jane Addams* and Florence Kelley.

Susan B. Anthony* Memorial House, Rochester.

Anthony* and her sister Mary grew up here and lived here together all their lives, except when Anthony travelled. There are other memorials to Anthony around the Rochester area.

Val-Kill, Eleanor Roosevelt* National Historic Site, Hyde Park.

The fieldstone cottage just over a mile from the Roosevelt mansion was built especially for Eleanor. She spent much of her time hereafter FDR's death ,often with her companion, Lorena Hickok. ER and a few friends started a short-lived furniture factory behind Val-Kill.

NORTH CAROLINA
Biltmore Industries, Asheville.

Edith Stuyvesant Dresser(1873-1958) established the Industries in 1901 to preserve the Old World wool manufacturing skills of area women.

SOUTH CAROLINA
Penn Center Historic District, St. Helena's Island.

The Penn School was founded by Laura Towne(1825-1901) and Ellen Murray and became the first school for freed slaves in the South. Charlotte Forten(1837-1914), the school's first black teacher, wrote vividly about her experiences here during the Civil War.

TEXAS
King Ranch, Kingsville.

Henrietta Chamberlain King(1832-1925) inherited a huge but debt-ridden ranch in 1885 and, over forty years, doubled its size to one million acres and her fortune to more than $5 million.

VIRGINIA
Virginia Randolph Cottage, Glenallen.

Randolph(1874?-1958), an African-American, was an educator and supervisor of Negro schools. She began her long career from this cottage.

WASHINGTON
Providence Academy, Vancouver.

Esther Pariseau, "Mother Joseph"(1823-1902), journeyed from her home in Montreal with a group of nuns to help care for the poor. She had learned woodworking skills from her father.
She designed, supervised construction and fashioned the chapel woodcarvings for the Academy. It is the earliest surviving building of those she completed and now serves as shops and offices.

"Watch awhile and you will see these dashing, noisy, happy, healthy girls grow calm, pale, sad . . . And why? They have awakened to the fact that they belong to a subject, degraded,ostracised class; that to fulfill their man appointed sphere, they can have no individual character, no life purpose, personal freedom, aim or ambition. They are simply to revolve around some man . . .The world will talk to you of the duties of wives and mothers and housekeepers, but all these incidental relations should ever be subordinated to the greater fact of womanhood. You may never be wives, or mothers, or housekeepers, but you will be women, therefore labor for the grander, more universal fact of your existence."
Elizabeth Cady Stanton*
Speech, 1870's

Historical Monuments

Thousands of statues, monuments and memorials exist around America to honor local women or women who have a local connection.

COLORADO
Statue of Florence Sabin*, State Department of Health Building, Boulder.

DISTRICT OF COLUMBIA
"The Woman Movement," Crypt, US Capitol.
Honors Lucretia Mott, Susan B. Anthony, and Elizabeth Cady Stanton. Adelaide Johnson(1859-1955), sculptor. Gift from the National Woman's Party and artist in 1921.

Role of Women Bay, Washington Cathedral.
Includes effigies, statues and stained glass windows.

Statue of Mary McCleod Bethune*, Lincoln Park.
17-foot statue with inscription of Bethune standing with black children.

HAWAII
Monument to Mother Marianne, Kalaupapa Leprosy Settlement, Molokai.
Honors Barbara Cope, a German-American nun who continued the work with lepers begun by Father Damien.

ILLINOIS
Monument to Mother Jones*, Union Miners' Cemetery, Mount Olive.
Monument to Emma Goldman, Forest Home Cemetery, Forest Park.

KANSAS
Statue, "Pioneer Woman," State House Grounds, Topeka.
Lilla Day Monroe, sculptor. Depicts a vigilant woman holding a rifle, guarding an infant and child.

LOUISIANA
Statue, Margaret Gaffney Haughery, Margaret Haughery Park, New Orleans.
Irish immigrant and philanthropist known as "The Bread Woman."
Statue depicts woman with her arm around a child.

MAINE
Monument to Edna St. Vincent Millay*, Camden.
Placed at the seacoast view which inspired lines in her poem "Renascence."

MARYLAND
Monument, "Angel of the Battlefield," Antietam.
Honors Clara Barton*.

MASSACHUSETTS
Monument to Anne Hutchinson*, State House Grounds, Springfield.
Religious leader, 1591-1643, shunned for her beliefs.

Monument to the Lowell mill girls, Lowell National Historic Site, Lowell.

MICHIGAN
Statue of Laura Smith Haviland, Adrian.
Abolitionist and humanitarian, 1808-1898. Haviland played an active role with the Underground Railroad and opened an integrated school in the late19th century. Statue depicts a seated figure holding a book called "A Woman's Life Work" with inscription.

MISSOURI
Monument to Otahki, Trail of Tears State Park, Cape Girardeau.
Daughter of Cherokee leader who died during the Trail of Tears forced march.

NEW YORK
Bronze doors, American Academy of Arts and Letters, New York City.
Dedicated to the female writers of America.

Grave of Margaret Cochran Corbin, Revolutionary War hero, West Point Cemetery.

Plaque quoting lines from "The New Colossus,"Statue of Liberty.
Jewish-American poet Emma Lazarus(1849-1887) wrote the famous poem which includes the lines inscribed on the plaque beginning: "Give me your tired, your poor . . ."

OKLAHOMA
Statue of Sagajawea, Tuba.
The only of several statues around the country to show the legendary Shoshone trail guide(c.1786-1812) alone.

RHODE ISLAND
Memorial to Ida Lewis, Newport.
Lewis(1842-1911) was a lighthouse keeper for many years and became famous for her rescues. Consists of an anchor crossed with oars and inscription.

"Whenever I feel myself inferior to everything about me, threatened by my own mediocrity, frightened by the discovery that a muscle is losing its strength, a desire its power, or a pain the keen edge of its bite, I can still hold up my head and say to myself: . . . .'Let me not forget that I am the daughter of a woman who bent her head, trembling, between the blades of a cactus, her wrinkled face full of ecstasy over the promise of a flower, a woman who herself never ceased to flower,untiringly, during three quarters of a century."
Colette*
Break of Day, 1928

As we come marching, marching, in the beauty of the day,
A million darkened kitchens, a thousand mill lofts gray,
Are touched with all the radiance that a sudden sun discloses,
For the people hear us singing: "Bread and roses! Bread and roses!"

As we come marching, marching, we battle too for men,
For they are women's children, and we mother them again.
Our lives shall not be sweated from birth until life closes;
Hearts starve as well as bodies; give us bread, but give us roses!

As we come marching, marching, unnumbered women dead
Go crying through our singing their ancient cry for bread.
Small art and love and beauty their drudging spirits knew.
Yes, it is bread we fight for--but we fight for roses, too!

As we come marching, marching, we bring the greater days.
The rising of the women means the rising of the race.
No more the drudge and idler--ten that toil where one reposes,
But a sharing of life's glories: Bread and roses! Bread and roses!

"Bread and Roses"
Words by James Oppenheim, c.1912

"It doesn't pay well to fight for what we believe in."
Lillian Hellman*
Watch on the Rhine, 1941

Literature

❝ It would have been impossible, completely and entirely,
for any woman to have written the plays of Shakespeare
in the age of Shakespeare.. . . [A]ny woman woman born with a great gift
in the sixteenth century would certainly have gone crazed, shot herself,
or ended her days in some lonely cottage outside the village,
half witch, half wizard, feared and mocked at. ❞
Virginia Woolf
A Room of One's Own*, 1929.

❝ What did it mean for a Black woman to be an artist in our grandmothers' time?
It is a question with an answer cruel enough to stop the blood. ❞
Alice Walker*
"In Search of our Mothers' Gardens,"1974.

Writers in English of Fiction & Drama

Women are important, even pivotal, in the development of the tradition of the novel in English.

Aphra Behn (1640-1689)
British. Among the first women to write professionally. A playwright and a pioneer of the novel, especially with the abolitionist novel *Oroonoko*(1688).

Jane Austen (1775-1817)
British. Inaugurated the tradition of women writing novels. Observer and critic of women's lives and conventions, for example with *Pride and Prejudice*(1813). Considered on a par with Shakespeare by many critics.

Mary Shelley (1797-1851)
British. The daughter of Mary Wollstonecraft is best known for her seminal science-fiction fantasy, *Frankenstein*(1818).

Harriet Beecher Stowe (1811-1896)
American. Her *Uncle Toms' Cabin*(1852) was a controversial sensation and watershed in abolitionist sentiment. Stowe also significantly advanced regional writing about New England.

Charlotte Brontë (1816-1855)
British. *Jane Eyre* (1848) was a best-seller and today is considered revolutionary for the independent spirit of its central female character.

George Eliot(Mary Anne Evans) (1819-1880)
British. Influenced the history and shape of the novel in her writing about everyday provincial life and its relation to public issues, especially with the semi-autobiographical *The Mill on the Floss*(1860).

Harriet E. Adams Wilson (c.1828-c.1860)
African-American. Her self-published *Our Nig* (1859)is the first known novel by a black American appearing in the US. The book chronicles the life of a free black in New England.

Louisa May Alcott (1832-1888)
American. Prolific writer of children's books, novels, and thrillers and an active suffragist.

Kate Chopin (1851-1904)
French Creole-Irish American. Chopin's reputation revived in the 1960s. Known for her recreations of southern French Creole life and especially women growing toward independence, as in *The Awakening*(1898).

Rosa Praed (1851-1935)
Australian. Prolific novelist who challenged the conventions of women's lives, as in the controversial *The Bond of Wedlock*(1887).

Olive Schreiner* (1855-1920)
Anglo-South African. Feminist and celebrity whose novels dramatize her pacifist and anti-imperialist sentiments, as in *The Story of an African Farm*(1883).

Edith Wharton (1862-1937)

American. Major figure in American literature. Her novels depict the life of privileged white society; *The House of Mirth,* 1905. Spent much of her life abroad.

Virginia Woolf(1882-1941)

British. Central figure in the famous Bloomsbury literary circle. Published much of her own work through her company Hogarth Press. Her fiction is celebrated for its innovative technique and feminist themes; *To the Lighthouse*, 1927.

Willa Cather (1873-1947)

American. Her novels often present powerful female characters, as in *O Pioneers!*(1913). Known especially for her writing about frontier life.

Isak Dinesen (Karen Dinesen Blixen)(1885-1962)

Danish. Storyteller *par excellence.* Especially remembered for her exquisite short stories which recapture the sensations of eras long past(*Babette's Feast*,1952). Also wrote in Danish.

Anzia Yezierska (c.1885-1970)

Jewish Polish-born American. A keen interpreter of the immigrant assimilation experience, as in *Bread Givers*(1925).

Katherine Mansfield (1888-1923)

New Zealand-born Briton. Her short stories about single women and precocious children have secured Mansfield's fame; *The Garden Party*, 1922.

Mourning Dove (hum-Ishu-Ma)(1888-1936)

Okanogan. First native American woman to write and publish. Remembered today for her Coyote Stories.

Nella Larsen (1893-1964)

African-American. A key novelist of the Harlem Renaissance and a pioneer in her treatment of black female sexuality; *Quicksand*, 1928.

Zora Neale Hurston (1901?-1960)

African-American. Folklorist and writer known today for her novels illustrating the richness and robustness of black culture, especially in *Their Eyes Were Watching God*(1937).

Christina Stead (1902-1983)

Australian. Novelist and screenwriter who spent much of her life in Europe and America. She has only recently been acknowledged in her own country as its greatest novelist; *The Man Who Loved Children*(1940).

Lillian Hellman* (1907-1984)

Jewish-American. A leading dramatist(*The Children's Hour*,1934) and, in later life, autobiographical writer. Admired for her declaration to the House Committee on Un-American Activities in 1952: *"I cannot and will not cut my conscience to fit this year's fashions."*

Eudora Welty (1909-)

American. Her novels of the rural South are noted for their engaging female characters; *The Optimist's Daughter*, 1972.

Hisaye Yamamoto (1921-)
Japanese-American. Highly regarded and widely-anthologized writer of short stories and pcems, especially depicting the Japanese-American experience(*Seventeen Syllables*, 1988).

Nadine Gordimer* (1923-)
Anglo-South African. Her many novels and short stories are read worldwide. She describes the complexities of life for English, Afrikaaner, and African residents of her country, and often exposes cruelty and hypocrisy. She writes eloquently about the South African landscape also; *Burger's Daughter*, 1978; *Crimes of Conscience*, 1991). Winner of the Nobel Prize for Literature.

Lorraine Hansberry (1930-1965)
African-American. Playwright, civil rights advocate and feminist remembered for her tragic death from cancer at 35, but enduringly for *A Raisin in the Sun*(1959) and *To Be Young, Gifted and Black*(1961, posthum.)

Toni Morrison (1931-)
African-American. One of the most gifted novelists writing today, Morrison records 20th century black American life, especially in the Midwest(*The Bluest Eye*, 1970; *Jazz*, 1992).

Margaret Atwood (1939-)
Canadian. First recognized internationally as a poet. Her popular novels address a wide range of themes including the environment, feminism, and Canadian national identity; *Surfacing*, 1972.

Alice Walker* (1944-)
African-American. Popular feminist writer who explores environmental, civil rights, and women's issues in her work(*The Color Purple*, 1982).

Louise Erdrich (1954-)
Turtle Island Chippewa-Irish American. Notable for her poetry as well as her fine novels portraying contemporary Native American life within the white culture(*Love Medicine*, 1984).

Ntokzake Shange (1948-)
African-American. Playwright of the black female experience, best-known for *"For Colored Girls Who Have Never Considered Suicide When the Rainbow is Enuf."*

"And it came to pass that after a time the artist was forgotten, but the work lived."
Olive Schreiner
The Artist's Secret

Writers of Fiction & Drama
Around the World

In many cultures, notably in Asia, the novel has no tradition among women writers or even among writers at large. Each country has its own tradition and esteemed writers, of which a few descriptions follow here.

George Sand(Amantine-Aurore-Lucile-Dupin) (1804-1876)
French. Internationally influential in her time, she was enormously prolific. Surviving works include more than 100 novels*(Lélia*, 1833) and thousands of letters. She defended sensual and idealistic love and her politics are a controversial theme among contemporary critics.

Gertrudis Gómez de Avellaneda (1814-1873)
Spanish/Cuban. Wrote poems, plays and novels, especially *Sab*(1841) in which she pointed out similarities between women and slaves as victims of society.

Emilia Pardo-Bazán (1851-1921)
Spanish. Influential critic, salonkeeper and novelist writing in realistic and later a spiritualistic style*(Los Pazos de Ulloa*-The Sons of the Bondswoman, 1886).

Grazia Deledda (1871-1936)
Italian. Winner of the Nobel Prize for Literature. Used the Sardinia of her youth as the setting for many of her thirty-odd novels. Focused on the inner dilemmas of characters*(La madre*-The Mother,1920).

Colette(Sidonie-Gabrielle Colette) (1873-1954)
French. Writer involved in many genres and other ventures but best known for her novels(*Chéri*, 1920). Her female characters are strong and sensuous. An exotic and unconventional figure in French society. Many novels have appeared in English to great success.

Margit Kaffka (1880-1918)
Hungarian. First great female writer claimed by her country. Her pioneering works of fiction are impressionistic narratives in which women face frustration in their search for new roles*(Két nyár*-Two summers, 1916).

Uno Chiyo (1897-   )
Japanese. A notorious figure in Japanese culture for her modern views and practices. Extremely successful with short stories, novellas, and novels, many of which are based on fact(*Ohan*, 1961).

Ding Ling (1902-86)
Chinese. Championed in America after she was "rehabilitated" after a long period of disgrace and imprisonment. Early in her career, wrote short stories and then novels noteworthy for their new-style female heroes, as in *Sha-fei nu-shih te jih-chi*(Diary of Miss Sophie, 1927).

Mariama Bâ (d.1981)
Islamic African. Groundbreaking novelist best known for *Une si Langue Lettre*(So Long a Letter, 1979, trans. 1981). Winner of the prestigious Japanese literary award, the Noma.

Silvina Bullrich (1915-   )
Argentinian. Popularly acclaimed for novels like *Mañana digo basta*(Tomorrow I'll Tell Them I've Had It, 1968). Writes in a spiritual style about her concern for socioeconomic equity.

Rosario Castellanos (1925-1974)

Mexican. Writes of the late 1930s in her home state of Chiapas and focuses often on women's barriers in communication and Indian-white conflict(*Balún-Canán*-The Nine Guardians, 1960). A key figure in feminist literary discussions.

Clarice Lispector (1925-1977)

Ukrainian-born Brazilian. A major novelist exploring existential themes related to women's experience and voice.

O Chŏng-hŭi (1947-)

Korean. One of the outstanding Korean writers of fiction in the twentieth century, writing primarily short stories. Her work is provocative and technically exquisite(*Pyolsa*-Words of Farewell, 1981).

Isabel Allende (1942-)

Chilean living in exile in Venezuela. The most successful of Latin American female novelists. She writes complex, but highly readable novels(*Eva Luna*, 1987, trans., 1988). Her family saga *La Casa de los Espiritus*-House of the Spirits, 1982, trans. 1985)was an instant bestseller in Latin America, Europe and the United States.

Buchi Emecheta(1944-)

Nigerian. First African writer to address feminism overtly. Her work is widely reviewed and critically acclaimed; *The Joys of Motherhood*, 1979).

Penina Muhardo(1948-)

Tanzanian. Writes by choice in Kiswahili on social and development issues. Playwright and novelist(*Nguzo-mama*-Mother Pillar,n.d.).

"Writing is keeping track of one's own being, especially in my own case. My first book is about my life, my mother's generation and so on. But it is also true that is very difficult to keep track. The problem is finding the time to put things down. A lot of women remember everything in their head, but they have no time to really sit down and write."

Buchi Emecheta*
Interview, *In Their Own Voices*, 1990

"I don't wish not to be a woman, but I'd certainly like to be a woman whose sense of purpose comes from within.

Uno Chiyo*
"Mohô no Tensai"(A Genius of Imitation), 1936

Poets Writing in English

Women of nearly every culture have used poetry to express themselves. Most cultures consider poetry acceptable for women, though not necessarily published poetry. The list of excellent female poets is very long and what follows gives just a sense of the worldwide participation.

Anne Bradstreet* (1612-1672)
British-born. America's first poet. She wrote personal, autobiographical poems about her life.

Emily Dickinson (1830-1886)
American. She allowed few poems to reach publication in her lifetime, and her complete works, numbering 1775 poems, were not published until 1955. Dickinson is now considered by many as the finest American poet.

Elizabeth Barrett Browning (1806-1861)
British. A major and highly prolific poet of the 19th century, also an active feminist and abolitionist. Her reputation as a sentimental poet is undergoing revision as feminist scholars study her entire body of work.

Frances E. W. Harper* (1825-1911)
African-American. She used verse to dramatize political commitments to feminism and the abolition of slavery.

Mary Elizabeth Coleridge (1861-1907)
British. Although overshadowed by ancestor Samuel Taylor Coleridge, her work, including several novels, is now well-regarded.

Dame Mary Gilmore (1865-1962)
Australian. A legend in Australia for her poetry and journalism, which expresses her interests in the needy and dispossessed.

Amy Lowell (1874-1925)
American. A major figure in the Imagist movement. She extended the influence of Imagism as a lecturer and reader. Her poems deal with mystical themes and idealization.

Gertrude Stein (1874-1946)
American. Expatriate living in France. A genius in many minds. She attempted to translate Cubism into poetry and wrote in other genres as well.

H.D.(Hilda Doolittle) (1886-1961)
American. Expatriate living in England. A founder of the Imagist movement in poetry, her reputation has grown considerably in the last 20 years.

Marianne Moore (1887-1972)
American. Highly praised, award-winning writer. Her poetry is precise and innovative, expressing her moral convictions and keen interest in nature.

Elizabeth Bishop (1911-1979)
American. Known for her visionary and meditative poetry. Bishop also wrote extensively on the nomadic life. She lived for long periods in Brazil.

Judith Wright(1915-   )
Australian. Writer in multiple genres known for her passionate attachment to the Australian landscape.

Gwendolyn Brooks (1917-   )
African-American. Throughout her long career, she has used Chicago as the background for her writing about the black disenfranchised. Her poetry is widely read at every level.

Kath Walker (1920-   )
Noonuccal Australian. First woman of Aboriginal descent to achieve fame as a poet. She is active in native rights and educational issues.

Adrienne Rich (1929-   )
American. Highly-regarded feminist/lesbian poet, activist, and writer. Her poetry has evolved in both form and content and today declares her strong political convictions.

Sylvia Plath (1932-1963)
American. A major contemporary poet also known for her autobiography, *The Bell Jar*(1971). All Plath's work records the emotional crises of her brief life.

Kamala Das (1934-   )
Indian. Her British writing reflects Indian cadences and themes. Known for her defiance of taboos placed on upper-class Indian women.

(Kareen)Fleur Adcock (1934-   )
New Zealander. This higly-regarded poet disconcerts readers by juxtaposing the bizarre and the everyday. The genteel tone of her work allows her to deal with taboo subjects.

Lucille Clifton (1936-   )
African-American. A prolific and exuberant poet, also known for her children's books. She often writes about her heritage and the impact of history on the individual.

Judy Grahn (1940-   )
American. Noted for her innovative form and writing on working-class and lesbian issues. She is irreverent and delights in exploring new forms suggested by other cultures.

Mitsuye Yamada (n.a.)
Japanese-American. California teacher and poet whose work spans forty years. She has written of the internment of Japanese-Americans during World War II and today tends to address the concerns of Asian-Pacific women.

I am obnoxious to each carping tongue
Who says my hand a needle better fits,
A poet's pen all scorn I should thus wrong.
For such despite they cast on female wits:
If what I do prove well, it won't advance,
They'll say it's stol'n, or else it was by chance.
Anne Bradstreet*
From *"The Prologue"*

Poets around the World

Most of the poets below are available in some English translations. The list suggests the strong tradition of women's poetry in many diverse cultures.

Sappho (6th century BC)
Greek. Poet of high reputation who taught other girls and women on the island of Lesbos. The term lesbian originates with her reputed lifestyle and love poetry.

Ts'ai Yen (c. 200 AD)
Chinese. The first great female poet of China.

Al-Khansâ (7th century AD)
Arab. Four pre-Islamic poets shared this name and wrote of woman's traditional role as ritual mourner.

Hroswitha (c.935-1005)
German. Prolific nun who wrote poems and plays in Latin. A Renaissance nun accomplished in a wide array of subjects, including science.

Princess Nukada (late 7th century)
Japanese. Considered the greatest among many women writing poetry during her time. In Japan, women authored most of the major contributions in literature before the modern era.

Li Ching-chao (1084-1151)
Chinese. Scholar and collector most highly esteemed among female poets.

Comtesse de Die (late 12th century)
French. Best-known of the *trobairitz*(female troubadours) writing between the 8th and 11th century.

Louise Labé (1525-1566)
French. A renowned poet and celebrity of the French Renaissance.

Mihri Hatun (d. 1506)
Turkish. Intellectual and first major female poet of the Ottoman Empire.

Hwang Chin-i (c. 1507-1544)
Most famous and talented of female poets of Korea.

Sor Juana Iñes de la Cruz (1652-1695)
Mexican. A great figure in Latin American literature, a nun and early feminist. She wrote sensuous poetry, as well as plays and an autobiography which defends women's learning.

Anne Maria Lenngren (1754-1819)
Distinguished as a translator also, Lenngren is considered the greatest pre-20th century Swedish woman writing poetry.

Kaga no Chiyo (1701-1775)
Japanese. Best known female writer of *haiku*.

Ho Xuan Huong (late 18th century)
Her poems are controversial because of their dealings with taboo subjects like sex and feminism, but this writer's work is part of the established literary canon of Vietnam.

Annette von Droste-Hülshoff *(1797-1848)
Most important German female poet of the 19th century.

Gertrude Gomez de Avellaneda (1814-1873)
Considered the national poet of Cuba in the late 19th century.

Anna Akhamatova (1889-1966)
One of the finest Russian poets of the 20th century, persecuted by Stalin. Her early concise, evocative poetry was transformed after her reinstatement to tragic Christian verse.

Gabriela Mistral* (Lucila Godey Alcaya) (1889-1957)
Chilean. Mistral was a teacher who became a UN delegate and worker for social justice. Best known for her emotional lyric poetry. Also authored novels on Chilean life.

Juana de Ibarbourou (1895-1979)
Uruguayan. Called Juana de Américas, highly influential in Spain and Latin America.

Katri Lala (1901-1944)
A major poet of Finland.

Leah Goldberg (1911-1970)
Israeli. Influential in the new Israel as a scholar and poet.

Julia de Burgos (1914-1953)
A major figure in Puerto Rican letters.

Anne Hébert (1916-)
French Canadian. Given the highest literary honors in Quebec. Author of two masterpieces of modern Canadian writing, both considered brilliant and profound(Le tombeau des rois, 1953; trans. The Tomb of Kings, 1967).

Fadwa Tuquan (1917-)
Palestinian(Jordan). One of the finest avant-garde writers in the Arab world.

Amrita Pritam (1919-)
Punjabi. A major figure in contemporary Indian literature.

Ishigaki Rin(1920-)
Japanese. Celebrated and popular poet whose work appears in Japanese newspapers.

Noémia da Sousa(1927-)
Portuguese(Mozambique). First black African women to gain recognition as a poet.

Jenny Mastoráki(1949-)
One of the outstanding new voices in Greek poetry.

Classics of Feminist Thought

Feminist ideas have circulated for several centuries and became widely known in the West by the 19th century. The early writers often focused on the need for women to be educated.

La Cité des Dames (The City of Ladies, c.1410)
Christine de Pisan(1364-1430). Italian-French. An unusually learned woman living at the time of Jeanne D'Arc. *Dames* records the accomplishments of women in past times. The earlier *Le livre des trois vertus*(Book of the Three Virtues) defends woman's right to education.

Vindication of the Rights of Women (1792)
Mary Wollstonecraft(1759-1797). British. This profoundly influential work challenges prevailing egalitarian arguments by applying them to women. Argues for equal education rights for all women and employment for single women.

Woman in the Nineteenth Century (1845)
Margaret Fuller (Ossoli)(1810-1850). American. Influential work advocating women's rights and especially the right of education.

Women and Economics (1898)
Charlotte Perkins Gilman(1860-1935). American. Attacks the idea that women must be financially dependent and proposes that woman's status is tied to their economic condition. Gilman also authored the classic tale *The Yellow Wallpaper*(1892) and the utopian novel, *Herland*(1915).

A Room of One's Own (1929)
Three Guineas (1938)
Virginia Woolf*. British. Classic works which address the obstructions to woman's achievement and commitment. The idea that women need personal space to achieve has been applied to nearly every aspect of feminist thought.

Le deuxième sexe (The Second Sex, 1949)
Simone de Beauvoir(1908-1986). Formidable two-volume study tracing the nature of female oppression through myth, history, political theory, and psychology. de Beauvoir later co-founded *Questions feministes*.

The Feminine Mystique (1963)
Betty Friedan(1921-). Jewish-American. One of the galvanizing factors in the second wave of feminism in America. *Mystique* identified the "problem that has no name": the pressure placed on women to conform to the role of housewife and mother.

Les guérillères (The Warriors,1969)
Questions feministes (1979-)
Monique Wittig(1944-). French. *Warriors* is a groundbreaking allegory of female resistance. The journal *Questions* was founded with de Beauvoir and Christine Delphy and assumed a high profile internationally on matters of theory.

"Reflections on the Black Woman's Role in the Community of Slaves" (1970)
Angela Davis(1944-). African-American. Pivotal article on the historical role of American black women, still widely quoted.

Sisterhood is Powerful: An Anthology of Writings
from the Women's Liberation Movement (1970)
Sisterhood is Global:
The International Women's Movement Anthology (1984)
Edited by Robin Morgan(1941-). Neither book is strictly theory. *Powerful* brought the articles of diverse activists from different perspectives to a large audience. *Global* introduced the views of feminists worldwide to American women.

Woman's Estate (1972)
Psychoanalysis and Feminism (1974)
Juliet Mitchell(1940-). New Zealand born-Briton. *Estate* analyzes the women's liberation movement from a Marxist perspective. *Feminism* advocates a diligent review and revision of patriarchal structures, with Freudian thought as a prime example.

Lesbian Nation: The Final Solution (1973)
Jill Johnston*(1929-). British-American. A classic wedding of lesbian and feminist identitiy.

Beyond God the Father (1973)
Gyn-Ecology (1979)
Mary Daly(1928-). American. A theological writer's perspective on patriarchal religions and the role of religion in contemporary society. The innovative use of language in *Gyn-Ecology* was highly influential.

Quest (journal,1974-1982)
Passionate Politics: Essays, 1968-1986 (1987)
Charlotte Bunch(1944-). American. Bunch has not achieved the fame of other theorists in America, partly because most of her writing is in article form and also because of her association with radical lesbian separatism early on. She is an outstanding thinker among feminists today and has increasingly turned her attention to global feminism.

Of Woman Born: Motherhood as Experience and Institution (1976)
Adrienne Rich*. A landmark exploration of the myth and the reality of motherhood.
Winner of the National Book Award.

A Black Feminist Statement (1977)
Combahee River Collective(a Boston group). Influential article outlining the genesis of Black feminism as well as issues and practice.

In a Different Voice (1982)
Carol Gilligan(1936-). American. Challenges the notion that the moral and ethical thinking of women is identical to that in men. *Voice* has been a controversial but powerful force in redirecting the development of ideas on female psychology.

This Bridge Called My Back (1983)
Edited by Cherríe Moraga(Chicana, 1952-) and Gloria Anzaldúa(Tejana Chicana, n.a). Groundbreaking collection of poetry,prose, narrative and analysis which extended American women's understanding of the diversity of ethnic and sexual identities among feminists of color.

Classics of Feminist Fiction and Autobiography

Many excellent novels, short stories and autobiographies have appeared in the last 20 years. Earlier works have been rediscovered. It is impossible to compile a "good" list of these books: inevitably many favorites are excluded. The listing below is primarily American work. The letters CA refer to coming-of-age books; CC designates a coming-to-a-new-consciousness theme; F refers to fiction; SF, science-fiction or fantasy; A, autobiography; AF, autobiographical fiction; G , anthology.

The Awakening
CF Kate Chopin*,1898.

The Yellow Wallpaper
AF Charlotte Perkins Gilman*, 1892

Daughter of Earth
AF-CC Agnes Smedley, 1929

Passing
AF Nella Larsen*, 1929

The Street
F Ann Petry, 1946

Their Eyes Were Watching God
F Zora Neale Hurston, 1937.

Brown Girl, Brownstones
A Paule Marshall, 1959.

I Know Why the Caged Bird Sings
CA-F Maya Angelou, 1969.

Memoirs of an Ex-Prom Queen
CA-F Alix Kates Shulman, 1972.

Sula
CC-F Toni Morrison*, 1973.

The Female Man
SF Joanna Russ, 1975.

Woman on the Edge of Time
SF Marge Piercy, 1976.

Diary of Anaïs Nin, 6 vols.
A Anaïs Nin, 1976.

The Woman Warrior: Memoirs of a Girlhood Among Ghosts
AF Maxine Hong Kingston*, 1976.

"Mother said I would grow up a wife and a slave, but she taught me the song of the warrior woman . . ."
Maxine Hong Kingston*
The Woman Warrior, 1976

Rubyfruit Jungle
AF Rita Mae Brown, 1977.

The Women's Room
A Marilyn French, 1977.

Final Payments
F Mary Gordon, 1978.

The Color Purple
CC-F Alice Walker*, 1982.

The Mists of Avalon
SF Marion Zimmer Bradley, 1982.

**Night Flying Woman:
An Ojibway Narrative**
A Ignatia Broker, 1983.

Love Medicine
F Louise Erdrich*, 1984.

The Land of Look Behind
CA-A Michelle Cliff, 1984.

The House on Mango Street
CA-F Sandra Cisneros, 1985.

Annie John
CA-F Jamaica Kincaid, 1985.

The Handmaid's Tale
SF Margaret Atwood, 1986.

When I am an Old Woman, I Shall Wear Purple
G Ed. Sandra Martz, 1987.

Seventeen Syllables and other stories
AF Hisaye Yamamoto, 1988.

The Forbidden Stitch: An Asian-American Women's Anthology
G Ed. S. G. Lim et al, 1989.

**Spider Woman's Granddaughters: Traditional Tales and
Contemporary Writing by Native American Women**
G Paula Gunn Allen, 1989.

*"I never said I was a dyke even to a dyke
because there wasn't a dyke in the land
who thought she should be a dyke
or even thought she was a dyke
so how could we talk about it."*
Jill Johnston*
Lesbian Nation, 1973

Mystery Women

Women have enjoyed great success with mystery-writing: Agatha Christie is the best-selling author of all time. It is probably not a coincidence that most of the protagonists below are independent women.

Miss Amelia Butterworth by Anna Katharine Green
1897-1917(6 books) American
Predecessor of Miss Jane Marple, Miss Butterworth embodies Victorian womanhood except for her strong talent for, and interest in, detective work.

Maud Silver by Patricia Wentworth (Dora Amy Elles Dillon Turnbull)
1928-1961(32 books) British
Miss Silver is a retired governess, a "paragon of respectability and morality."
She works
professionally as a private detective.

Adela Beatrice LeStrange Bradley by Gladys Mitchell
1929-1985(68 books) British
Ms. Bradley is a woman of advanced age and experience, thrice-wed with grown children. The author hints that her ancestors include a long line of witches. She works as a consulting psychiatrist to the Home Office.

Nurse Sarah Keate by Mignon Eberhart
1929-1954(7 books) American
Nurse Keate works as a private duty nurse and becomes involved with melodramatic searches for murderers.

Miss Jane Marple by Agatha Christie
1930-1987(19 books) British
The quintessential little old lady is a "wonderful houseguest" who solves all the mysteries coming her way with grace, perseverance, and logic.

Rachel and Jennifer Murdock by D. B. Olsen (Dolores Hitchens)
1939-1956(13 books) American
Two middle-aged sisters live in Los Angeles and approach their lives and the mysteries they find with great gusto. Titles in the series always refer in some way to cats.

Abbie Harris by Amber Dean
1944-1954(8 books) American
Set in a lakeside village in upstate New York, this series concerns a widow in her early 40s who lives with her sister. Many World War II-era themes are explored.

Julia Probyn by Ann Bridge (Lady Mary Dolling O'Malley)
1956-1973(10 books) British
Julia Probyn is a free-lance journalist of whom her Scottish relatives don't quite approve.

Charmian Daniels by Jennie Melville (Gwendoline Butler)
1962-1981(8 books)
Charmian Daniels is the only series in which a British policewoman operates in the provinces. The provincial setting is unprecedented for policewomen/detectives.

Kate Fansler by Amanda Cross (Carolyn Heilbrun)
1964-1986(8 books) American
Kate Fansler is a professor of literature at a New York City university(much like the author) and marries during the course of the series.

Mrs. Emily Pollifax by Dorothy Gilman
1966-1985(7 books) American
The widowed Mrs. Pollifax appears as an agent for the Secret Service in these deceptively simple stories.

Tessa Crichton by Anne Morice (Felicity Shaw)
1970-1987(20 books) British
Tessa Crichton is a London-based actor married to a Scotland Yard Chief Inspector. Her voluble character is known for dry wit.

Norah Mulcahaney NYPD by Lillian O'Donnell
1972-1987(12 books) American
Detective Mulcahaney has moved up the police force ladder to be homicide detective. She marries and becomes widowed during the series.

Mrs. Charles by Mignon Warner
1976-1984(7 books) British
The chameleon-like hero of the series uses several aliases, including that of a clairvoyant. She is middle-aged and lives with a half-brother. As much mystery exists inside the character of Mrs. Charles as outside it.

Sharon McCone by Marcia Muller
1977-1985(7 books) American
Sharon McCone is a sociology student in the San Francisco area forced by unemployment into investigative work. She works as the staff detective for the "All Souls Legal Cooperative."

Charlotte Ellison by Anne Perry
1979-1987(8 books) British
Ms. Ellison, like many of her sister sleuths, has a "startling inquisitiveness and honest outspoken nature" which sometimes embarrasses her upper-class British family.

V.I. Warshawski by Sara Paretsky
1982-1988(5 books) American
One of the least attractive personalities in mystery series. Some readers find Chicagoan V.I. too abrasive for their taste. She recently surfaced in a film bearing her name.

> " . . . with the satisfied fervour of one who has at last pinned a label on a rare specimen.
> 'She is, of course, one of your typical English spinsters.' . . .
> 'I suppose she has given up?'
> 'Given up what?' "
> Doris Lessing
> *"Our Friend Judith,"*
> *A Man and Two Women*, 1958

Best-Sellers

A best-seller is a book which sells more than 100,000 copies in hardcover and 1 million in paper. Here is a partial listing of best-sellers by female authors.

1905   **The House of Mirth**
1921   **The Age of Innocence**
Edith Wharton*

1930   **Mythology**
Edith Hamilton(1867-1963). American.

1938/39   **The Yearling**
Marjorie Kinnan Rawlings*

1939   **Gone With the Wind**
Historical novel by Margaret Mitchell(1900-1949). American.

1952   **The Diary of Anne Frank**
Anne Frank(1929-1945). German-Jewish.

1960   **To Kill A Mockingbird**
Harper Lee(1926-). American.

1966   **Five Smooth Stones**
Interracial romance set in the civil rights era.
Ann Fairbairn(Dorothy Tait) (1902?-1972). American.

1966   **The Mask of Apollo**
One of many Renault historical novels about ancient Greece;
she was a trained classicist.
Mary Renault(1905-1983).

1968   **Testimony of Two Men**
Historical novel,one of many Caldwell best-sellers.
Taylor Caldwell(1900-1985). American.

1969   **The Three Daughters of Madame Liang**
Buck lived much of her life in China and wrote about it often.
Pearl S. Buck*.

1970   **Losing Battles**
Eudora Welty*.

1970   **The Crystal Cave**
Many of Stewarts' novels are best-sellers, including the so-called
Merlin trilogy, of which this book is the first.
Mary Stewart(1916-). British.

1971   **Nemesis(a Jane Marple mystery)**
Christie's 95 books have sold more than 500 million copies.
Agatha Christie(1890-1976). British.

1971   **The Bell Jar**
Autobiographical fiction.
Sylvia Plath*.

1972   **The Happy Hooker**
Xaviera Hollander1936?-). Dutch-American.

1973   **I Heard the Owl Call My Name**
A fictional priest's encounter with Native Americans of the
contemporary northwest.
Margaret Craven(1901-1980).

1975   **Looking for Mr. Goodbar**
Fact-based contemporary novel, later a movie.
Judith Rossner(1935-). American.

1977   **Delta of Venus: Erotica**
An early entry into erotic literature through a woman's eyes.
Anaïs Nin(1903-1977). French-American.

1977   **The Women's Room**
Feminist autobiography.
Marilyn French(1929-). American.

1979   **Hanta Yo**
Novel about Dakotah tribal existence between 1794 and 1835,
for which the author researched for 25 years.
Ruth Beebe Hill(n.a.). American.

1980   **Fanny**
A feminist reinterpretation of the classic erotic novel.
Erica Jong(1942-). American.

1981   **Spring Moon**
Novel about a Chinese family, 1892-1970s.
Bette Bao Lord(1938-). Chinese-American.

1982   **The Valley of Horses**
Prehistoric feminist adventure.
Jean Auel(1936-).

1984   **...And Ladies of the Club**
A lifetime in the making, this novel depicts the lives of members
of a woman's club in small town Ohio, 1868-1932.
Helen Hooven Santmyer(1895-1986), American.

The Nobel Prize for Literature

Alfred Nobel, the inventor of nitroglycerine and dynamite, bequeathed his entire estate in 1901 as an investment to generate funds for five annual prizes of outstanding achievement. Today ,the Nobels are among the most prestigious awards in the world. Critics have noted that the judging is not immune from political and personal concerns. Winners now receive about $200,000. Women comprise 5% of all Nobel winners(24 of 458 awards since 1901). American women are seven of the 24 female winners in all categories.

1909 Selma Lagerlöf* (1858-1940)
Swedish. Lagerlöf was disabled from childhood. She gained fame from her writings on the folklore of her home region of Sweden, especially *The Story of Gösta Berling*(1891).

1926 Grazia Deledda*
Italian. Signora Deledda won the Nobel for novels such as *La Madre*(The Mother,1920), and *Canne al Vento*(Reeds in the Wind), notable for their lyric naturalism.

1928 Sigrid Undset (1882-1949)
Norwegian. Undset is remembered today for *Kristin Lavransdatter(1921-22),* her epic novel on life in medieval Norway. She won also for novels of modern life such as *Jenny(*1928).

1938 Pearl S. Buck* (1892-1973)
American. Spent much her youth in China. Buck wrote *The Good Earth*(1931) about a peasant family in China. She is also remembered for her advocacy of stronger US-China relations, and equality of opportunity for all races and abilities.

1945 Gabriela Mistral*
The celebrated lyrical genius of Spanish literature. She has become a symbol of her country's nationalist aspirations.

1966 Nelly Sachs (1891-1970)
German-born Swedish citizen. Sachs fled with her family to Sweden when the Nazis targeted the Jews for extermination. Her later poetry spoke eloquently of the experience.

1991 Nadine Gordimer*
Gordimer's selection may be attributed partially to the worldwide pressure on South African to modernize its social system. Gordimer writes movingly about the situation in her homeland.

"Thinking is never so easy as when one follows a plow up a furrow and down a furrow."
Selma Lagerlöf*
Jerusalem, 1915

Performing Arts

❝ *If your soul can soar above technique and float in the lofty regions of creative art,
you have fulfilled your mission as a singer. For what mission can be greater
than that of giving to the world hours of exaltation in which it may forget
the misery of the present, the cares of everyday life and lose itself
in the eternally pure world of harmony . . .*❞
Lotte Lehmann*
More Than Singing, 1945

❝ *All my life, even when after years had brought me the seemingly unattainable,
I have found in women's affection a peculiar understanding, a mothering quality
that is a thing apart. Perhaps too I had a foreknowledge of the difficulties that
in a world arranged by man for man's convenience beset the woman who leaves
the traditional path to compete for bread and butter, honours and emoluments . . .
The people who have helped me most at difficult moments of my musical career
have been members of my own sex.* ❞
Ethel Smyth*
Impressions That Remained, 1918

Classical Composers, Conductors, & Musicians

The "women's field" in music is performing and especially singing; the quintessentially male field is conducting. A singer appears to bend herself to the will of the audience, but the conductor must communicate authority at all times. The women below have struggled against the odds to achieve in the musical field of their choice.

Hildegard of Bingen (1098-1178)
German. A woman of many different talents, Hildegard's music has only recently received attention. One collected volume includes more than 77 pieces of music. She wrote the earliest surviving liturgical morality play, which predates any other by 200 years.

Madalena Casulena (c.1540-c.1590)
Italian. Composer, teacher, singer and musician known for her madrigal compositions.

Elisabeth-Claude Jacquet de la Guerre (c.1666-1729)
French. Composer and musician whose works include opera.

Clara Wieck Schumann (1819-1896)
German. A leading pianist of her day, considered the peer of Liszt and Anton Rubinstein. One of the first solo concert artists to perform without accompanying musicians. Also a composer and teacher.

Luise Adolpha Le Beau (1850-1927)
German. Pianist, music critic, and composer of more than 66 works including chamber music.

Ethel Smyth (1858-1944)
British. Internationally recognized as a composer of opera(*The Boatswain's Mate*, 1913), Smyth was a *bon vivant*, suffragist and advocate for women musicians.

Amy Cheney Beach (1867-1943)
American. First American woman to achieve an international reputation as a composer of many types of classical music. Beach wrote the first major American symphony.

Nadia Juliette Boulanger (1887-1979)
French. The "world's greatest composition teacher" is considered to have had the greatest influence on American music composition through students like Gershwin and Copland. Also a symphony conductor and organist.

Florence B. Smith Price (1888-1953)
African-American. The first black woman to win recognition as an American composer. Her symphonies have been performed by major orchestras.

Ethel Leginska (1886-1970)
British. The leading British pianist of her day and the first woman to conduct leading American symphony orchestras. Leginska also organized several women's orchestras.

Ruth Crawford Seeger (1901-1957)
American. An innovative modernist composer who also helped to preserve American folk songs through her transcriptions and arrangements. Mother of folk singer-songwriter Peggy Seeger.

Philippa Duke Schuyler (1932-1967)
African-American. A child prodigy who was composing at age 3 and debuting with the New York Philharmonic at age 14. A world-touring guest soloist on the piano.

Sarah Caldwell (1924-)
American. Producer of opera, conductor of major Armerican symphonies and founder of the Boston Opera Group. Currently artistic director and conductor of the Group, now the Opera Company of Boston.

Tania Justina Leon (1944-   )
Cuban. A piano soloist with top orchestras in the 1970s and later, the musical director of the Dance Theatre of Harlem.

"The conductor and director must create the atmosphere, but a situation must exist where the singers can think and use their own remarkable faculties. It's like bringing up a gifted child."
Sarah Caldwell
Ms., 1975

Popular Musicians, Composers, & Conductors

Teodore Gines (16th century) *"Ma Teodora"*
African-Dominican. The first female composer in the Americas.
A minstrel performer and orchestra leader.

Fanny Crosby (1820-1915)
American. Prolific composer of 8500 hymns, despite her blindness from infancy.

Queen Liliuokalani (1838-1917)
Hawaiian. Composer of over 100 songs including the Hawaiian national(now state) anthem.

Carrie Jacobs-Bond (1862-1946)
American. The most successful female songwriter of her day who had to start her own music
publishing company to obtain recognition. Her compositions included *I Love You Truly*(1906).

Maria Grever (1885-1951)
Mexican. First woman in her country to gain fame as a composer. Grever worked in a variety of
fields, including film scoring and pop(*What a Difference a Day Makes*).

Valaida Snow (c.1900-1956) *"Queen of the Trumpet"*
African-American. Bandleader and performer especially popular throughout Europe.

Malvina Reynolds (1900-1978)
American. Gifted singer-songwriter who voiced her concerns on many social issues,
who wrote *Little Boxes*(1962) and *What Have They Done to the Rain?*(1962).

Dorothy Fields (1905-1974)
American. Lyricist responsible for hundreds of popular and jazz standards, including the lyrics
for the musical *Sweet Charity*(1965).

Mary Lou Williams (1910-1981)
African-American. Outstanding jazz pianist, composer, and arranger who established her own
record company. Remembered for her jazz mass, *Music for Peace*(1969).

Hazel Scott (1920-1981)
Trinidad-born American. A child prodigy, this acclaimed pianist is known for
"swinging the classics."

Toshiko Akoyoshi (1929-)
Japanese, living in US. Highly-regarded jazz composer, bandleader and keyboardist.

"Any woman who has a great deal to offer the world is in trouble.
And if she's a black woman, she's in deep trouble."
Hazel Scott
Ms., 1974

Familiar Songs Composed by Women

Battle Hymn of the Republic
Lyrics by Julia Ward Howe.

America, the Beautiful
Lyrics by Katherine Lee Bates.

I Love You Truly (1906)
Words and music by Carrie Jacobs-Bond.

Don't Blame Me (1932)
The Way You Look Tonight (1936)
Big Spender (1965)
Words by Dorothy Fields.

Willow Weep for Me (1932)
Words and music by Ann Ronell.

Aloha Oe (1939)
Words and music by Queen Liliuokalani.

God Bless the Child (1941)
Words and music by Billie Holiday(with Arthur Herzog, Jr.).

Turn Around (1958)
What Have They Done To The Rain? (1962)
Words and music by Malvina Reynolds.

Up on the Roof (1963)
Words and music by Carole King(and Gerry Coffin).

Both Sides Now (1967)
Big Yellow Taxi (1970)
Words and music by Joni Mitchell.

Until It's Time for You to Go (1968)
Words and music by Buffy Sainte-Marie.

Stone Soul Picnic (1968)
Words and music by Laura Nyro.

From A Distance (1990)
Words and music by Julie Gold.

Song Stylists

Elizabeth Taylor-Greenfield (c.1820-1876)
African-American. The first black concert singer, Taylor-Greenfield was born in slavery and largely self-taught. Her voice was considered astonishing and her vocal range was an incredible 3 1/2 octaves.

Jenny Lind (1820-1887) *"The Swedish Nightingale"*
Swedish. A legendary concert singer and opera star whose career began at the age of 10. She was "admired to distraction " and toured internationally. The only woman represented in Westminster Abbey's Poets' Corner.

Sissieretta Jones (1869-1933)
African-American. Highly-acclaimed concert and popular singer who was also a star of the musical theatre.

Lotte Lehmann (1888-1976)
German. International opera star.

Adelina Patti (c.1860-1919)
Italian-American. Opera and concert singer prominent in the late 1800's.

Bessie Smith (1895-1937) *"Empress of the Blues"*
African-American. The first female jazz star, known for her "cast-iron contralto" and her bridging of country and classic blues. Her untimely death from medical neglect was caused by the segregated hospital system of the South; the incident became the subject of a play by Edward Albee.

Mabel Mercer (1900-1984)
African-British. Influential jazz star, much-admired for her highly individual style.

Marian Anderson (1902-) *"The Voice of the Century"*
African-American. Legendary operatic and concert diva and, in 1954, the first black to sing at the Metropolitan Opera.

Edith Piaf (1915-1963)
French. Fabled dusky-voiced cabaret singer who created lyrics for many of her own songs, such as *La vie en rose*(1947).

Judy Garland (1922-1969)
American. Actor and concert performer whose personal troubles became as famous as her tremulous voice.

Maria Callas (1923-1977)
American-born Greek. Though minimally trained, she is considered one of the greatest operatic sopranos of the 20th century. Remembered as much for her perfectionist attitude and her colorful private life.

Sarah Vaughn (1924-1990) *"The Divine One"*
African-American. Incomparable jazz stylist whose voice and technique improved with age.

Leontyne Price (1927-)

African-American. Distinguished international operatic soprano whose voice is described as "like a bright banner unfurling." Noted for her interpretations of Verdi's leading roles.

Nellie Melba (1861-1931)

Australian. Concert and opera star and one of the few powerful enough to dictate casting decisions. Completed more than150 recordings. Her fame is recorded for posterity in two food names: *melba toast* and *peach melba.*

Patsy Cline (1932-1963)

American. The enduring queen of country music, whose reputation continues to grow.

Miriam Makeba (1932-) *"Mama Africa"*

Black South African. Internationally acclaimed singer and prominent anti-apartheid activist. Exiled from her country for more than 30 years, she travels the world on honorary passports.

Buffy Sainte-Marie (1941-)

Cree-Canadian. Considered by some to have the greatest scope of female folksingers.
Known in America for her umcompromising protest songs of the 60's and 70's(*Universal Soldier,* 1963), but also an accomplished pop songwriter(*Until It's Time for You to Go,* 1968).

Tania Maria (1942-)

Brazilian. Inventive singer, pianist and composer who blends Brazilian pop with American jazz.

Barbra Streisand (1942-) *"The Voice"*

Jewish-American. Multi-talented vocalist, actor, director and composer known for her musical comedy roles(*Funny Girl*, 1965) and her avoidance of live performance.

Joni Mitchell* (1943-)

American. Celebrated singer-songwriter whose folk songs and singing have gradually moved toward jazz.

Janis Joplin (1943-1970)

American. A rock legend and one of the few white singers to succeed with the combination of rough edges, emotional toughness and vulnerability characteristic of the great black blues singers like Bessie Smith.

Joan Armatrading (1947-)

West Indian-British. Much-admired singer and guitarist, especially popular in Britain. Known for her imaginative styling and overtly feminist lyrics.

Bonnie Raitt (1949-)

American. Increasingly prominent singer-songwriter who has embraced blues, jazz, country and pop styles during her career. Highly-regarded also for her virtuosity on the guitar.

Holly Near (1949?-)

American. Popular singer-songwriter in feminist circles. Perhaps bes tknown for her collaborations with Ronnie Gilbert, formerly of The Weavers. Near frequently addresses social and political issues in her songs.

Dancers & Choreographers

Lucille Grahn (1819-1907)
Danish. Internationally-known ballerina who, in later life, achieved fame as a choreographer for the opera.

Virginia Zucchi (1849-1930)
Italian. Prominent ballerina who toured throughout Russia and Europe. A major influence on Russian dance and noteworthy for her extraordinary skill as a technician.

Ruth St. Denis (Dennis) (1877-1968)
A popular solo dancer, a foremother of modern dance, whose specialty was exotic settings.

Isadora Duncan (1879-1927)
American. Her expressive dancing anticipated modern dance. Her performances were thought magnetic and inspiring.

Anna Pavlova (1882-1931)
Russian, later living in London. Internationally-acclaimed prima ballerina known for her dedication, technique, and magnetic appeal.

La Argentina (Antonia Mercé) (1888-1936)
Spanish. A prima ballerina at 11 years of age. Her fame as a child prodigy blossomed into acclaim for the concert artist who specialized in regional Spanish dance and a distinctive castanet style.

Martha Graham (1894-1992)
American. Dancer and choreographer of renown remembered for her highly original work, including dances expressing the experience of women, as in *Letter to the World*.

Helen Tamiris (Helen Becker) (1902?-1966)
Russian-Jewish American. A prime mover in modern dance as both dancer and choreographer. Also a developer of social dances and a Broadway choreographer.

Peggy van Praagh (1910-)
Briton, living in Australia. An influential figure in Australian dance performance and education as a ballet dancer, teacher, and producer.

Margot Fonteyn (Peggy Hookham) (1919-)
British. Outstanding prima ballerina known as a superb interpreter of classic roles. The first British ballerina of international stature, she was still performing at age 62.

Pearl Primus (1919-)
Trinidadian, living in Nigeria and the US. Dancer and choreographer known for ritualistic dance.

Agnes de Mille (1908-)
The pre-eminent Broadway choreographer for many years, she is honored for bringing ballet into the musical theatre.

Judith Jamison (1943-   )
African-American. Much-celebrated soloist for the Alvin Ailey Dance Troupe and known for her passion and presence on stage. Now directs the Ailey Troupe.

Twyla Tharp (1942-   )
American. One of the most original and innovative choreographers. Early works were unaccompanied by music but vibrant and seemingly spontaneous. Later, she utilized jazz to develop a virtuoso style.

Suzanne Farrell (1945-   )
American. Considered the leading interpreter of George Balanchine's work. Soloed at the New York City Ballet at 17.

"As is the case in all branches of art, success depends in a very large measure upon individual initiative and exertion, and cannot be achieved except by dint of hard work. Even after having reached perfection, a ballerina may never indulge in idleness."
Anna Pavlova*
Quoted in *Pavlova: A Biography*, 1956

"When I listened to music the rays and vibrations of the music streamed to this one fount of light within me--there they reflected themselves in Spiritual Vision, not the brain's mirror, but the soul's, and from the vision I could express them in Dance."
Isadora Duncan*
My Life, 1927

"The truest expression of a people is in its dances and its music. Bodies never lie."
Agnes de Mille*
NY Times Magazine, 1975

Feature Filmmakers

Women have always made films, from the earliest days of the technology. Women making films were seldom acknowledged until they gained new visibility with the women's movement of the 1970's and the search for foremothers. Often, female filmmakers have chosen to bring women's experiences to the center of their work, even though the "woman's film" historically draws a small audience. The recent surprise success of Thelma and Louise*(1991) may change that history.*

Alice Guy-Blache (1875-1968)
French, later living in America. The world's first female film director. Probably the first person to tell a story on film. Also a pioneer in both aesthetic and technical areas. Worked on films in France, Spain, and America.

Elvira Notari (1875-1946)
Italian. The earliest and most prolific female director in Italy. She formed her own company and co-wrote many short films, directing in a style ahead of her time; for instance, she often used location shoots.

Olga Preobrazhenskaia (1881-1971)
Russian. The most important woman in Russian-Soviet cinema. She worked as an actor before becoming her country's first female director;*Baby riazanskie,*1927).

Lois Weber (1881-1939)
American. Her fame as a director in the 1910's rivalled Cecil de Mille's. Her salary probably exceeded his. Her entire work includes hundreds of silent films. She is notable for sensitive treatments of moral dilemmas.

Germaine Dulac (1882-1942)
French. The most important and prolific French director between 1920 and 1930. The mother of surrealism in film. Dulac's controversial surrealist *La Coquille et le Clergyman*(The Seashell and the Clergyman,1927) preceded Dali's *Le Chien andalou* by two years.

Dorothy Arzner (1900-1979)
American. The first American female director to bridge the silent and sound eras and the first woman successful at directing cinema. Her *Christopher Strong*(1933) written by Zoë Akins and starring Katharine Hepburn has been described as "the intelligent woman's primal post-coital scene"(Pauline Kael).

Pauline McDonagh (1901-1978)
Australian. A pioneer director. Worked with two sisters to make films like *The Cheaters*(1930), which were wholly different from the Australian films of their time.

Muriel Box (1905-   )
British. Screenwriter/director working in partnership with husband Sydney. Among her most successful films is *The Seventh Veil*(1945).

Ida Lupino (1918-1991)
British-born American. All-around filmmaker(actor, screenwriter, musician) and one of the few women directing in the Hollywood studios of the 1950s. Specialized in mass entertainment features and in later life directed episodes of many television dramatic and action shows; *The Hitchhiker*(1952).

Mai Zetterling (1925-)
Swedish. Actor, later director and screenwriter; *The Girls*(1968).

Agnes Varda (1928-)
Belgian-born French. "Mother of the New Wave" of French filmmaking. Once considered the finest woman directing films in the world; *Le Bonheur*(Happiness, 1965).

Véra Chytilová (1929-)
Czech. Part of the Czech New Wave, her style emphasizes improvisation. She often uses non-actors for authenticity. Best known for *Daisies*(1966), an anarchic and feminist film originally banned from release in her land.

Marta Meszaros (1931-)
Hungarian. Internationally-recognized director whose films tend to focus on the aspirations and daily struggles of women, as in *Diary for My Children*(1984).

Maria Luisa Bemberg (1940-)
Argentine. One of the few filmmakers from her country whose work is distributed internationally. She always works with executive producer Lita Stantic and focuses on women's obstacles to independence.

Joan Micklin Silver(1935-)
Jewish-American. Prolific director of film, television and Broadway. She often deals with women's sexuality and problems of maturity. The highly unusual *Hester Street*(1975) was black-and-white and in Yiddish. Silver returned to similar subject matter in *Crossing Delancey*(1988).

Claudia Weill(1947-)
American. Started working as a camerawoman and then turned to documentary filmmaking (*Joyce at 34*, 1973). An early feature film, *Girlfriends*(1978) was a forerunner in films examining feminist issues.

"As an artist, I cannot situate myself among those who complain.
If we are going to create, or to re-create the sources of women's self-expression,
I believe they will not be plaintive . . . I want to illuminate women's lives--not only their hardships,
although they're important, but also the light, the transparence, the pleasure of being a woman."
Agnes Varda
Quoted in *Ms.*, 1978

Independent Filmmakers

*Some women have chosen the freer path of filmmaking outside feature film circles. Others use short or documentary filmmaking as training for feature films. Of particular note for short films by women is Studio D, the women's unit of the National Film Board of Canada. Studio D has mothered many outstanding films including the anti-pornography **Not a Love Story**(1980) and **Goddess Remembered**(1985). Women Make Movies in New York City is the only American distributor of films and videos made by women.*

Maya Deren (1917-1961)
Russian-American. The mother of the US avant-garde film. Noteworthy for her success with independent distribution and her thematic experiments with personal fantasy, as in *At Land*(1944).

Beryl Fox (1931-)
Canadian. Documentary filmmaker(*The Double Standard*, 1963) gradually moving into the making of features.

Yvonne Rainer (1934-)
American. An accomplished dancer and later independent filmmaker. Her work is multi-layered and often dense. Her particular interest is in power relationships, as in *Kristina Talking Pictures*(1976).

Barbara Hammer (1939-)
American. Highly visible independent filmmaker concentrating on feminist-lesbian theme; *Women I Love*, 1979.

Valie Export (1940-)
Austrian. Enjoys an international reputation for avant-garde films, especially concerning the socialization surrounding the female form(*Menstruations film*, 1967).

Abigail Child (1948-)
American. Documentary, short, and avant-garde filmmaker and a central figure in New York City's avant-garde film movement; *Mayhen,*1987.

Ayoka Chenzira (195?-)
African-American. Multitalented maker of films and videos. Her animated satire, *Hairpiece: A Film for Nappy-Headed People* (1987) concerned racist standards of beauty.

Julie Dash (1952-)
African-American. Has focused on black women's image and self-definition in short films and in her first acclaimed feature, *Daughters of the Dust*(1992).

Trinh T Minh-Ha (1953-)
Vietnamese-American. Independent writer, composer and filmmaker. Works with ethnographic and documentary films. Invented the "subjective documentary." Her *Surname Viet Given Name Nam*(1989) looks at the role of women in Vietnamese culture.

Feature Films about Women's Lives

It is still unusual to find a film which examines the world through women's eyes. So-called women's films have appeared throughout the history of cinema--most in America are independent short films or documentaries and do not find a large audience.

Sunshine Sally (1922-Australia)(silent)
A early film examining woman's status.

La Souriante Madame Beudet (The Smiling Mme. Beudet, 1923-France)
Directed by Germaine Dulac*. A film "of vibrant feminism" about the fantasies and frustrations of a middle-aged woman.

Erba Jiaren (Beautiful Sixteen, 1927-China)
Directed by Zheng Zhengqiu. A silent melodrama addressing the barriers to women's education.

The Truth About Women (1958-England)
Directed by Muriel Box*, written with Sydney Box. Considered a strike for equal rights for women.

Loving Couples (1964-Sweden)
Directed by Mai Zetterling*. Taken from a Swedish novel by Agnes von Krusenstjerna. Three women and their search for independence in society.

Rachel, Rachel* (1968-United States)
Directed by Paul Newman. A moving portrait of middle age for a woman on her own, starring Joanne Woodward*.

L'Une chante l'autre pas (One Sings the Other Doesn't, 1977-France)
Directed and written by Agnes Varga*. Chronicles the friendship of two women.

The Turning Point (1977-US)
Directed by Herbert Ross. Two former ballet rivals reunite. Stars Anne Bancroft and Shirley MacLaine.

An Unmarried Woman* (1978-US)
Written and directed by Paul Mazursky. A woman struggles to recover her life after her husband walks out. Jill Clayburgh* in a star-making performance.

Norma Rae* (1979-US)
Directed by Martin Ritt. Fact-based drama about a cotton mill worker gaining political consciousness and leadership skills. Starring Sally Field*.

My Brilliant Career* (1979-Australia)
Directed by Gillian Armstrong from the 1901 novel by (Ms.)Miles Franklin, screenplay by Eleanor Witcombe. Energetic account of a poor farm girl's realization that to become a successful writer she will have to forego domestic bliss. Judy Davis* stars.

Nine to Five (1980-US)
Directed by Colin Higgins. An entertaining satire and farce which succeeds in making serious points about the status of clerical workers. Starring Lily Tomlin, Jane Fonda, and Dolly Parton.

Personal Best (1982-US)

Directed by Robert Towne. Two women in training for the Olympics fall in love. Noteworthy for its matter-of-fact consideration of the lesbian relationship. Stars Mariel Hemingway and Patrice Donnelly.

Entre Nous (1983-France)

French film directed by Diane Kurys. Two women become friends and eventually leave their marriages to live with each other. Superb performances by Isabelle Huppert and Miou-Miou. Oscar-nominated for best foreign film.

Visages de femmes (Faces of Women, 1985-Ivory Coast)

Directed by Désiré Ecaré. Traces the intertwined lives of three different women.

I've Heard the Mermaids Singing (1987-Canada)

Directed by Patricia Rozema. One of an increasing number of woman-centered feature films by Canadian women.

The Accused* (1988-US)

Directed by Jonathan Kaplan. A gripping drama examining the dynamics of rape and its aftermath. Starring Jodie Foster*.

Gorillas in the Mist* (1988)

Directed by Michael Apted. An uncompromising fact-based portrayal of the life and career of primatologist Dian Fossey*. Screenplay adapted by Anna Hamilton Phelan and Tab Murphy. Starring Sigourney Weaver*.

A Cry in the Dark* (1988-Australia)

Directed by Fred Schepisi. Fact-based drama which focuses on how the Australian public indicted a woman perceived to be responding in an "unwomanly" fashion to the disappearance of her infant. Starring Meryl Streep*.

Thelma and Louise* (1991-US)

Directed by Ridley Scott. Oscar-winning screenplay by Callie Khouri. Two friends plan a brief vacation together which becomes a flight for acceptance and independence.

"The idea that acting is quintessentially 'feminine' carries with it a barely perceptible sneer, a suggestion that it is not the noblest or most dignified of professions. Acting is role-playing, role-playing is lying, and lying is a woman's game."
Molly Haskell
From Reverence to Rape, 1987

Substantial Women in the Movies

Women have many opportunities to act in film, but their roles are severely limited in type and range. This is especially true for women of color. We have yet to see a nonstereotypical Native American woman on screen and are just beginning to see Hispanic and African-American women in substantial roles in feature films.

Mae West in **She Done Him Wrong** (1933)

Claudette Colbert in **It Happened One Night** (1934)

Bette Davis in **Jezebel** (1938)

Rosalind Russell in **His Girl Friday** (1939)

Greta Garbo in **Ninotchka** (1939)

Ethel Waters in **Cabin in the Sky** (1943)

Ingrid Bergman in **Casablanca** (1943)

Katharine Hepburn in **Adam's Rib** (1949)

Judy Holliday in **Born Yesterday** (1950)

Katharine Hepburn in **The African Queen** (1951)

Joanne Woodward* in **The Three Faces of Eve** (1957)

Claudia McNeil in **A Raisin in the Sun** *(1961)

Anne Bancroft and Patty Duke in **The Miracle Worker** *(1962)

Joanne Woodward* in **Rachel, Rachel** *(1968)

Jane Fonda in **They Shoot Horses, Don't They** (1969)

Glenda Jackson in **Women in Love** (1970)

Diana Ross in **Lady Sings the Blues** (1972)

Cicely Tyson in **Sounder** (1972)

Glenda Jackson in **A Touch of Class** (1972)

Jessica Lange in **Frances** (1972)

Ellen Burstyn in ***Alice Doesn't Live Here Anymore*** (1974)

Simone Signoret in ***Madame Rosa*** (1978)

Sally Field* in ***Norma Rae*** *(1979)

Sigourney Weaver* in ***Alien*** (1979)

Judy Davis* in ***My Brilliant Career****(1980)

Jill Clayburgh* in ***An Unmarried Woman*** *(1980)

Jane Alexander in ***Testament*** (1983)

Whoopi Goldberg in ***The Color Purple*** (1985)

Kathleen Turner in ***Prizzi's Honor*** (1985)

Geraldine Page in ***The Trip to Bountiful*** (1985)

Sissy Spacek in ***Violets are Blue*** (1986)

Marlee Matlin in ***Children of a Lesser God*** (1986)

Meryl Streep* in ***A Cry in the Dark*** *(1988)

Jodie Foster* in ***The Accused*** *(1988)

Glenne Headly in ***Dirty Rotten Scoundrels*** (1988)

Sigourney Weaver* in ***Gorillas in the Mist*** *(1988)

Melanie Griffith in ***Working Girl*** (1988)

Barbara Hershey in ***A World Apart*** (1988)

Jessica Tandy in ***Driving Miss Daisy*** (1989)

Susan Sarandon and Gena Davis in ***Thelma and Louise*** *(1991)

Philosophy
&
Science

❝ *In every known society, the male's need for achievement can be recognized.*
Men may cook, or weave, or dress dolls or hunt hummingbirds,
but if such activities are appropriate occupations of men, then the whole society,
men and women alike, votes them as important. When the same occupations
are performed by women, they are regarded as less important. ❞
Margaret Mead*
Male and Female, 1948

❝ *For women there are, undoubtably, great difficulties in the path,*
but so much the more to overcome! First, no woman should say,
'I am but a woman!' But a woman! What more can you ask to be? ❞
Maria Mitchell*
Address, 1874

Anthropologists

Anthropology is the study of human origins, cultures and development. The people-centered nature of the field tends to attract women, but the fieldwork necessary in sometimes distant locales is an obstacle for many. Women have participated in anthropology since before its creation as a separate field of inquiry in the 1800's.

Erminnie Adele Platt Smith (1836-1886)

American. First woman to practice field ethnography(written descriptions of a culture). She recorded the legends of the Six Nations of the Iroquois federation tribes of New York State. Although an amateur before the professionalization of the field, she was considered gifted.

Daisy Bates (1863-1951)

Irish. Also working before anthropology became formalized, she spent much of her life among the Australian aborigines, whom she brought to the attention of anthropologists; *The Passing of the Aborigines*,1938.

Elsie Clews Parsons (1875-1941)

American. Influential, nonconformist social anthropologist and folklorist. Her fieldwork focused on the tribes of the American Southwest. She worked to gather black American and Caribbean folk tales as well.

Ella Cara Deloria (1888-1971)

Yankton Dakota. Linguist and anthropologist who recorded the best material available on Dakota culture. Her particular interest was the language and myths of the traditional culture.

María Cadilla de Martínez (pseud. 'Liana') (1886-1951)

Puerto Rican. Multi-talented folklorist and writer who worked to recreate and preserve the traditional culture of her heritage, especially customs, tales, and children's songs. One of the first Puerto Rican feminists.

Hortense Powdermaker (1896-1970)

German-Jewish-American. Much-admired teacher and a pioneer in studies of the American South, Hollywood and contemporary Africa.

Ruth Benedict* (1887-1948)

American. Influential conceptual anthropologist, as in her *Patterns of Culture*(1934). Completed fieldwork with the tribes of the American Southwest and on the Pacific Islands. Attacked the bases of racism in 1940 with *Race: Science and Politics*. A towering figure in the history of anthropology.

Margaret Mead* (1901-1977)

American. One of the first anthropologists to make use of film and photography. Her signal contribution is considered to be rendering the field accessible to laypeople and convincing them of its importance in understanding their own society. An international figure. Author of over 40 books including *Coming of Age in Samoa*(1928) and *Blackberry Winter: My Earlier Years*(1962).

Jane Goodall (1934-   )

British. Zoologist famous for her work with the chimpanzees around Lake Tanganyika; *In the Shadow of Man*, 1971. Inspired by her work with Louis Leakey and internationally acclaimed for her work of many decades in Africa.

Dian Fossey* (1932-1985)

American. She met the Leakeys and Jane Goodall and was inspired to study the mountain gorilla of East Africa. She virtually lived with gorillas for 18 years and became a passionate and controversial anti-poaching advocate. Fossey was murdered in 1985. Her book *Gorillas in the Mist* (1983) and the film of the same name (1985) document her life with the gorillas.

Peggy R. Sanday (c.1938-   )

American. Teaching and prominent scholar in the areas of cognitive and mathematical anthropology, particularly with regard to American minority groups.

Karen Sacks (c.1945-   )

American. Sacks' particular interest is in the status of women and how it is affected by social and economic change. She is one of a group of contemporary feminist anthropologists who are in the process of redefining the field by examining culture from women's perspective. Also active in the women's movement.

"Work even when I'm satisfied with it is never my child I love nor my servant I've brought to heel. It's always busy work I do with my left hand, and part of me watches grudging the wastes of a lifetime."
Ruth Benedict
Quoted in *An Anthropologist At Work*, 1951

Archaeologists

Excavations are literally the stuff of archaeology. Since excavation sites tended until recently to be remote--a journey more aptly called an expedition--the idea of women in archaeology was an uncomfortable one. Nevertheless, women have participated, albeit in small numbers, since the amateur days of the field.

Madame de Cristol (early 19th century)
French. A pioneer in the new field of archaeology, who found evidence of tools and extinct animals in the caves of southern France.

Sophie Schliemann (late 19th century)
Greek. Chosen to assist her husband Heinrich in excavating the lost city of Troy, she came to be considered the more diligent of the pair.

Margaret Murray (1863-1963)
British. Linguist, researcher, ardent feminist, and popular writer who became involved with Egyptology in her early career. Her influential *The Witch Cult in Western Europe* is now considered controversial.

Hetty Goldman (1881-1972)
American. First woman to lead an officially-sanctioned expedition from the American School of Classical Studies. Her reputation as a researcher is distinguished. In the days before archaeology was professionalized, she was involved with excavations in Asia Minor, Greece, Turkey and Yugoslavia.

Gertrude Caton-Thompson (1888-   )
British. An early professional of high repute in England. Involved in significant excavations and discoveries in Egypt, Zimbabwe, and Arabia.

Florence Hawley Ellis (1906-   )
American. During a career spanning 50 years, she focused on the Pueblo and Navaho tribes of New Mexico, gained the tribes' trust, and became one of the earliest scholars permitted to work on forbidden tribal sites.

Kathleen Mary Kenyon (1906-   )
British. She proposed one of the two main theories of the 1950s on the origins of agriculture, was director of the British School of Archaeology in Jerusalem and directed an extensive excavation at Jericho.

Dorothy Cross Jensen (1906-1972)
American. Career of more than 40 years. Her early publications on the Near East were highly-regarded. Most of her work has focused on the New Jersey area. She headed a site survey during the Depression, which became the raw material for her later work.

Frederica de Laguna (1906-)
American. Organized and led expeditions to Alaska and led pioneering studies in a virtually unknown setting. Her work has provided eye-opening information on the prehistory and contemporary culture of the Eskimos and the Athabaskans.

Marjorie Ferguson Lambert (1910-   )

Scottish-American. The first woman to occupy a major curatorial position and an authority on the dating of artifacts. Performed excavations of Pueblo sites.

Mary Nicol Leakey (c.1910-   )

British. Mary and Louis Leakey were one of the best-known teams in Old World archaeology. They made significant contributions to knowledge of the history of early man in their long-term research on the Kenya-Tanzania border. Mary Leakey's contributions to the research were more greatly acknowledged after their divorce and Louis' death in 1972.

Hannah Marie Wormington (1914-   )

French-American. A leader in the field of Paleo-Indian or Early Man archaeology. Her text on the prehistoric tribes of southwest America became the premiere text on the subject for 20 years.

Marian Emily White (c. 1926-)

American. A leader in archaeology and a forerunner in using statistics in the field. Her special interest was the pre- and ethnohistory of the Iroquois Confederacy and the Seneca Nation; she was known for her excellent relations with the tribes, for hiring their youth, and protecting tribal sites.

Marija Gimbutas (1921-   )

Lithuanian-born American. She has specialized in Bronze and Iron Age sites in Eastern Europe, an area only recently accessible to scholars from the West. She has authored books on what archaelogists now know related to goddess-worship.

Germaine Henri-Martin (c.1950-)

French. As a young professional, she made the surprising discovery of *homo sapien* remains below the usual range at a site in Fontechevade.

"The deeper the archaeologists dig, the further back go the origins of man and society--and the less sure we are that civilization has followed the steady upward course so thoroughly believed in by the Victorians. It is more likely that the greatest civilizations of the past are yet to be discovered."
Elizabeth Gould Davis
The First Sex, 1971

Astronomers

As in most fields, women historically were given positions of low prestige and pay in astronomy . Unlike other fields, the duties accorded women allowed them to make important contributions to the advancement of astronomical knowledge.

Aganice(Athyrta) (2000+ BC)

Egyptian. Living well before the development of astronomy as a science, she was known for her use of celestial globes and the study of constellations to predict the future.

Elisabeth Korpmann Hevelius (1600's)

Polish. In partnership with her husband, she completed the largest star catalog compiled without the aid of a telescope.

Maria Winkelman (1671-1720)

German. The most outstanding of many female astronomers in her country. She managed an observatory and produced an astronomical calendar for the Berlin Academy.

Nicole-Reine Étable de la Brière Lepaute (1723-1788)

French. Her marriage to the royal clockmaker resulted in her becoming one of the best "astronomical computers" of the day. Worked on calculating the orbit of Halley's comet to predict its return and also successfully calculated eclipses. A crater on the moon bears her name.

Caroline Herschel (1750-1848)

German-British. With her brother William, founded sidereal astronomy(the study of stars) and advanced the field to the study of star systems. Discovered 2500 new nebulae and star clusters in partnership with William. Honored throughout the Europe of her day as a distinguished astronomer.

Maria Mitchell* (1818-1889)

American. As a talented amateur, discovered a comet while observing the sky on her rooftop in Nantucket.
Later became the first director of the Vassar College Observatory and, by creating opportunities for students, became a major influence on women's participation in the field.

Mary Whitney* (1847-1921)

American. Successor to Mitchell and her former student. Used her excellent mathematical skills to take on ambitious projects like the calculating of orbits. Also involved with observation of double stars, asteroids, and comets. Actively promoted women's education.

Williamina Fleming (1857-1911)

Scottish-American. Began as a housekeeper to the director of the Harvard Observatory and without formal degrees developed a classification system for stars. The work, categorizing over 10,000 stars, was published in 1890. Considered the leading female astronomer of the day. Her study of stellar spectra plates resulted in her discovery of 10 of the 24 novae ever recorded up to 1911.

Antonia Maury (1866-1952)

American of Portuguese descent. Another Mitchell student who discovered the second double star and contributed to the understanding of the phenomenon. She later became the first to compute periods of revolution for the component stars of the two double stars.

Annie Jump Cannon* (1863-1941) *"The Census Taker of the Sky"*
American. Developed the definitive system for classifying stars and proved that most stars represent only a few species. Established a prize bearing her name with the funds from one of her many awards. some suggest that her tremendous achievements stem in part from an ability to concentrate which was an outgrowth of her deafness. Worked from the age of 23 at Harvard Observatory.

Henrietta Leavitt (1868-1921)
American. Also deaf, she spent her life working at the Harvard Observatory. Her discovery involving the constellation Cepheid made possible investigations of the Milky Way galaxy. She also discovered 2400 variable stars of which only half were known at the time.

Cecilia Payne-Gaposchkin (1900-1979)
British-American. Her dissertation on the history of 20th-century astronomy was thought brilliant. She continued her distinguished research career, publishing more than 150 papers and four books. Her research examined the spectra of large, luminous stars and types of variable stars. Her contributions were not so much in data collection, as were some of the women listed above, but in the synthesis of available data.

"A life spent in the routine of science need not destroy the attractive human element of a woman's nature."
Annie Jump Cannon*
Quoted in *Science* magazine, 1911

"I hope when I get to heaven I shall not find the women playing second fiddle."
Mary Whitney*

Biologists

Biology is one of the oldest sciences and women have entered biology more so than any other science. Since biologists study living things, this science attracted more women or appeared more acceptable to other people. While women's work has advanced the field, few names are recognizable.

Margaretta Hare Morris (1797-1867)
American. Naturalist whose work with the 17-year locust and Hessian fly was instrumental in controlling these carriers of devastation. First woman to be given membership in the Philadelphia Academy of Science.

Ethel Browne (1885-1965)
American. Specialty was the field of differentiation and development. Her volume on sea urchin embryology in 1956 is still the standard reference in the field. Her work never was recognized with a full faculty position.

Libbie A. Hyman (1888-1969)
American. Early work on developmental biology and taxonomy. Her life's work was a five-volume treatise on *The Invertebrates*(1940-1967). The book was acclaimed internationally and remains the primary resource in the field of invertebrate zoology. Published her last volume at age 78.

Nettie M. Stevens (1861-1912)
American. During her brief professional career of nine years(post Ph.D.), she gathered definitive proof that the chromosome is the basis of sex determination. Also the first to demonstrate regeneration in the flatworm and the first to describe the chromosome of the European vinegar fly(the model species for studying genetic inheritance).

Katharine Foot (b. 1852) and Ella Strobell (d.1920)
American. Virtually unknown collaborators who were never affiliated with an institution and possibly funded their own research. The first to take photos through the microscope, they worked out many technical problems with the process. Their invention removed the subjectivity of the viewer from microscope research and thus raised considerably the level of work possible.

Barbara McClintock (1902-1992)
American. Much of her long career of work on genetic theory is now considered classic. Her work with Indian corn and subsequent revolutionary theory of gene functioning("jumping genes") took the scientific world 35 years to acknowledge with the Nobel Prize.

Rosalind Franklin (1920-1958)
Jewish-Briton. Outstanding biophysicist who made major contributions to studies of coal, DNA, and plant viruses. Perhaps best known for the controversy over credit for the solution of the structure of DNA. Her death at 38 from cancer ended a career many thought brilliant.

Rosalyn Sussman Yalow* (1921-   )
German-American. Used a Ph.D. in nuclear physics to work with medical application of radioisotopes. Working with Solomon Berson, she developed a method of measuring substances like drugs and hormones in the body. Yalow and Berson were awarded the Nobel Prize for their work.

Ida Hyde (1854-1945)

German-American. Her major contribution to the development of the microelectrode(useful in studying nerve and muscle fibers) has become invisible. Also made valuable contributions to neurobiology and vigorously advocated equal scientific opportunities for women.

Rita Levi-Montalcini (1909-   )

Jewish-Italian. Because of her status as a Jew in Mussolini's Italy, some of L-M's early work was clandestine. She discovered "nerve growth factor," a substance which keeps nerves from degenerating and plays a vital role in understanding how nerves work and the role of chemicals in controlling human development. Her work with Stanley Cohen was awarded the Nobel Prize in 1987.

Rachel Carson* (1907-1964)

American. Pioneer environmentalist. Biologist and naturalist whose writings describing the physics, chemistry, and biology of the ocean and shore engineered a wave of new consciousness about human interdependence with nature. Her book about the danger of DDT(*Silent Spring*, 1962) resulted in a ban on the use of DDT as an insecticide.

"Over increasingly large areas of the United States, spring now comes unheralded by the return of the buds, and the early mornings are strangely silent where once they were filled with the beauty of bird song."
Rachel Carson*
Silent Spring, 1962

"We cannot expect in the immediate future that all women who seek it will achieve full equality of opportunity. But if women are to start moving towards that goal, we must believe ourselves or no one else will believe in us; we must match our aspirations with the competence, courage and determination to succeed."
Rosalyn Yalow*
Quoted in *The Decade of Women*, 1980

Medical Scientists, Physicians & Nurses

Women apparently were often physicians in ancient times; we now call this type of medicine homeopathy or natural healing. In the 19th century, even midwives were excluded as medicine became more professional. The establishment of nursing effectively placed women in a permanently subsidiary role, with few exceptions until recently.

Dorothea Dix* (1802-1887)

American. Brought British social reform methods to the US in order to ensure separate housing for the mentally ill and criminals. Played a direct role in the founding of 32 mental hospitals. During the Civil War, served as Chief of Nurses for the Union. Developed the Army Nursing Corps.

Florence Nightingale* (1820-1910)

British. Founder of modern nursing as a result of her experiences nursing soldiers during the Crimean War. Also a pioneer in the use of statistical analysis of populations to address health problems.

Clara Barton* (1821-1912)

American. Spent her own money and volunteered to nurse Civil War soldiers and distribute provisions. Then served as Head Nurse of a two-corps army and organized corps hospitals. These experiences led her into a speaking career and much acclaim as a war heroine. She later established the American Red Cross(1881) and served as its president until 1904.

Mary Putnam Jacobi (1842-1906)

American. Remembered for her work opposing the prevailing medical opinion that the process of menstruation incapacitated women.

Alice Hamilton (1869-1970)

American. Invented the field of industrial medicine. Became especially involved in public health research and advocacy on hazards such as lead, arsenic and radium. Long-time associate of Jane Addams.

Florence Rena Sabin*(1871-1953)

American. First woman elected to the National Academy of Science. She accomplished significant work on lymphatic vessels, on tuberculosis, and later on public health problems like sewage disposal. The outstanding American female medical scientist of the early twentieth century.

Cicely Williams (1893-   )

Jamaican. During her 20 years working in West Africa, the first to describe the disease *kwashiorkor* (protein-calorie malnutrition), a leading and unnecessary cause of death in infants and children. Later the first head of Maternal and Child Health for the World Health Organization, among other positions. Published extensively on nutritional problems and child health in developing nations.

Mary Calderone (1904-   )

American. A forerunner in the development of responsible sex education for children as the co-founder of SIECUS(Sex Information and Education Council of the US). She believes in a continuum of sex education appropriate to age level. Also active in public health areas, including a stint as medical director of national Planned Parenthood from 1953-1964.

Virginia Apgar (1909-1974)
American. Invented a method for assessing the physiological status of newborns, called the Apgar score. Her method is the easiest and best means of evaluating infants and is widely used.

Katherine Sanford (1915-   )
American. Researcher at the National Cancer Institute throughout a long career. First person to clone a mammalian cell. Her work laid the foundation for the development of less cumbersome ways to achieve cloning. Cloning makes possible the development of vaccines and virus cultures and the study of many metabolic diseases.

Elisabeth Kübler-Ross (1926-   )
Swiss-American. The psychiatrist who pioneered a field ignored by traditional medicine. She was the first to introduce the dying patient's perspective to the public and the medical establishmen with *On Death and Dying*(1969).

Jane C. Wright(c.1922-
African-American. Pioneered the use of chemotherapy of tumors. At one time, served as Director of the Harlem Hospital Cancer Research Foundation.

"No man, not even a doctor, ever gives any other definition of what a nurse should be than this--'devoted and obedient.' This definition would do just as well for a porter. It might even do for a horse. It would not do for a policeman. . . . Merely looking at the sick is not observing."
Florence Nightingale*
Notes on Nursing, 1859

"In a world where there is so much to be done, I felt strongly impressed that there must be something for me to do."
Dorothea Dix*
Letters from New York, 1852

Philosophers

Since the debate over whether women should be educated at all continued for centuries, it is not surprising that women have limited visibility in a field which studies the source and nature of knowledge itself.

Aspasia (c. 470-410 BC)
Roman. A prostitute who lived with Pericles and is thought to have strongly influenced Socrates. Influential in an intellectual circle that included Socrates as well as Plato and Sophocles.

Hypatia (370-415 BC)
Greek. Teacher and director of the Neoplatonic School in Thebes at the age of 25 and an important proponent of Plato's philosophy. Author of mathemetical manuscripts as well and a martyr for her controversial views.

Pan Chao (c.45-120 AD)
Chinese. Scholar and philosopher concerned with the theory and practice of ethics; especially in *Nu Chien*(Lessons for Women).

Battista da Montefeltro Malatesta (1383-1450)
Italian. Celebrated for her unusually level of learning, she was a highly-admired teacher of philosophy.

Mary Astell (1666-1731)
British. Aligned with the Cambridge Platonists. Advocate of equal educational rights for women. Believed that Cartesian philosophy fostered self-consciousness and growth of woman's self-esteem.

Anne Finch Conway (1631-1679)
British. Proposed an early form of vitalistic philosophy and is thought to have influenced Leibniz greatly. Her philosophy anticipated evolutionary theory.

Emilie du Châtelet-Lomont (1706-1749)
French. Famous for her long-time liaison with Voltaire, she presented novel ideas in opposition to Descartes and Newton which were well ahead of her time. Also a translator of Newton.

Margaret Fuller* (Ossoli) (1810-1850)
American. Key member of the Transcendentalist circle around Boston. As journalist and writer, she was just achieving maturity as a thinker when she perished in a shipwreck.

Susan Stebbing (1885-1943)
American. Connected Aristotelian and symbolic logic.

Susanne Langer* (1895-1985)
American. Believed that symbolism was the key to all mental life; *Mind: An Essay on Human Feeling*(1967-72). She made important contributions in the field of linguistic analysis and aesthetics. Also a university teacher and lecturer.

Marjorie Glicksman Grene (1910-)

American. Made a significant impact on the philosophy of biology and evolutionary theory.

Hannah Arendt (1906-1975)

German-born American. Also a political theorist. Especially concerned with the nature of evil and the preconditions for thinking, willing, and judging, especially as concerns the causes of Nazism in Germany; *The Origins of Totalitarianism*(1951).

G.E.M. Anscombe (1919-)

British. Most distinguished female philosopher from England and a leader in linguistic philosophy. Her particular interests are logic, semantics, and the theory of language; *Three Philosophers*, 1961. Professor at Oxford and Cambridge.

Mary Warnock (1924-)

British. An existentialist concerned with empirical ethics. Makes a historical connection between Cartesianism and Sartre's theories. Her particular interest is the study of imagination.

"Feeling, in the broad sense of whatever is felt in any way, as sensory stimulus or inward tension, pain, emotion or intent, is the mark of mentality."
Susanne Langer*
Mind: An Essay on Human Feeling, 1967

"What woman needs is not as a woman to act or rule, but as a nature to grow, as an intellect to discern, as a soul to live freely and unimpeded, to unfold such powers as were given her when we left our common home."
Margaret Fuller*
Woman in the 19th Century, 1845

Physicists

Women are and have been active in all areas of physics; unlike other sciences, no area is considered the "woman's field." The percentage of female physicists is low but they have contributed to theory, experimentation, and all other areas.

Marie Curie* (1867-1934)

French. Her fame stems from two Nobel Prizes and a television movie of her life. A pioneer in experiments involving radioactivity. Discovered radium and polonium. Worked on early medical applications of radioactivity. Her daughter Irène Joliot-Curie continued her mother's work and also won the Nobel Prize.

Lise Meitner (1878-1968)

German-Jewish. A key scientist in both experimental and theoretical nuclear physics and chemistry in the early years of these fields. Discovered thorium C and protactinium with Otto Hahn and with C. D. Ellis, worked out the nature and properties of gamma and beta radiation.

Emmy Noether (1882-1935)

German-Jewish. One of the earliest women in 20th century physics, trained as a mathematician and theoretical physicist. "Noether's theorem" plays a central role in modern elementary particle physics and is taught to all students in modern field theory classes.

Katharine Burr Blodgett (1898-1979)

American. The first woman hired at General Electric's Research Lab, she invented nonglare glass and holds other patents involving film deposits on glass. Her work was groundbreaking and led to many other advances in the use of glass. She also worked on problems of tungsten lamp filaments and de-icing of aircraft wings.

Maria Goeppert-Mayer (1906-1972)

German-American. Awarded the Nobel Prize for her discovery of the role of spin-orbit forces in the shell model. Her thesis and a text on statistical mechanics are classics. Given little recognition until late in life.

Chien-Shiung Wu (1913-   )

Asian-American. Outstanding in modern experimental nuclear physics and in elementary particle physics, completing much of her work at Columbia University. Highly regarded among physicists for her experiments in the quantum field and on the theory of electromagnetism.

Mary Beth Stearns (1925-   )

American. Principal scientist on the science research staff at General Atomic and at Ford Motor Company. Contributions in solid-state physics and especially the area of magnetism.

"I was taught that the way of progress is neither swift nor easy."
Marie Curie
Pierre Curie, 1923

The Nobel Prizes in Science

Honors were given beginning in 1901 in Chemistry, Physics, and Physiology/Medicine.
Prizes supposedly are bestowed without regard to nationality; recipients must be living.
Marie Curie and Irène Joliot-Curie are the only mother and daughter to have received separate
awards. The Curie family has won five awards (Marie Curie, two(one with husband Pierre); Irène,
one with her husband). All awards were for the discovery of and continuing work on radioactivity.
Barbara McClintock was the only woman to receive a solo award in Physiology/Medicine.

1903 Marie Curie*   Physics
Awarded Curie, her husband and another colleague. The Curie research team
discovered polonism and radium.

1911 Marie Curie   Chemistry
Curie's husband Pierre died in 1906; she assumed his position at the Sorbonne.

1935 Irène Joliot-Curie (1897-1956)   Chemistry
French. Awarded jointly to Joliot-Curie and husband. Joliot-Curie continued her parents' work on
radioactivity, producing the first artificial radioactive substances.

1947 Gerty T. Cori (1896-1957)   Physiology/Medicine
Czech-born American. Awarded jointly with husband. Cori and her husband were innovators in
biochemistry in the areas of carbohydrate metabolism and enzymes.

1963 Maria Goeppert Mayer   Physics
Joint award. Team award for research on the structure of the atom and its nucleus.

1964 Dorothy Crowfoot Hodgkin(1910-) Chemistry
British. Hodgkin's analysis of crystals revealed the structure of penicillin, vitamin B-12
and other substances through X-ray technology. She later described the structure of insulin,
providing a boost to diabetes research.

1977 Rosalyn Sussman Yalow*   Physiology/Medicine
Jewish-American. Joint award. Team developed "RIA," an efficient method of measuring the
substances in blood.

1983 Barbara McClintock*   Physiology/Medicine
American. The only woman to receive the Physiology/Medicine prize solo. Given for her discovery
of mobile genes in the chromosomes of a plant which alter the plant's future generations.

1986 Rita Levi-Montalcini*   Physiology/Medicine
Joint award. For contributions to the understanding of substances that influence cell growth.

1988 Gertrude B. Elion(c.1917-)   Physiology/Medicine
American. Joint prize. Given for team discoveries of important principles for drug treatment.

Sports
&
Adventure

She was a big tough woman,
the first to come along,
That showed me that being female
meant you could still be strong.
And though graduation meant that we had to part
She'll always be a player on the ballfield of my heart.
From "Ode to a Gym Teacher"
Words and music by Meg Christian

❝ *Few such moments of exhilaration can come*
as that which stands at the threshold of wild travel. ❞
Gertrude Bell(1868-1926)
Syria

Athletes

What could be more unladylike than sports? In the days when women were expected to cover themselves from neck to toe and to look fragile, it took the courage of a pioneer to step out on a golf or tennis course or, heaven forbid, lift weights! The criticism of unwomanliness doubtless restrained many women from exploring their potential on the playing field.

Suzanne Lenglen (1899-1938)
French. Possibly the best female tennis player of all time. Winner of five Wimbledon titles and many national championships. Dominated amateur women's tennis from 1919-1926 and remembered for her highly emotional play.

Eleanora Sears (c.1905)
American. Multi-talented athlete who excelled at a variety of sports, including squash, tennis, polo and long distance walking. America's first well-known sportswoman, who loved the unusual.

Gertrude Ederle (1906-) *"Queen of the Waves"*
American. She swam the British Channel in 1925 in record time for any previous athlete. Held 18 world distance records in swimming at the age of 17. Won three Olympic medals.

Mildred Didrikson Zaharias* (1914-1956) *"Babe"*
American of Norwegian heritage. Probably the greatest athlete ever for her amazing skill,versatility, and unparalleled success. Winner of Olympic medals in track. She later turned to professional golf, but also tried her hand at swimming, tennis and boxing, and softball. Tragically dead from cancer at 42.

Patty Berg (1918-)
American. Her golf career spanned four decades. She won 29 amateur and more than 57 professional titles. Defined, along with Babe Didrikson, women's pro golf.

Florence Chadwick (1919-)
American. Her swimming career lasted 40 years. She was the first to break Ederle's Channel crossing record and later achieved a "grand slam" of four Channel crossings in five weeks, all record times.

Althea Gibson* (1927-)
African-American. Versatile athlete who broke the color barrier in both the US Lawn Tennis Association and later the Ladies' Professional Golf Association(LPGA player's card). Currently involved in state sports organizing in New Jersey.

Maureen Connolly* (1934-69) *"Little Mo"*
American. Dominated women's tennis until an accident forced her to retire at age 20. At age 17, became the first woman to win the Grand Slam(first place at the US, British, French, and Australian Opens in a single year). Dead of cancer at age 34.

Tamara Press (1937-)
Russian. Set 12 world records for shot put and discus throwing between 1959 and 1965. Competed in three Olympics, winning six medals(five of them gold). Sister Irina, also a world-class athlete, competed in track.

Wilma Rudolph (1940-   ) *"The Gazelle"*
African-American. First woman to win three gold medals in Olympic track(1960). Later turned to coaching and teaching.

Billie Jean (Moffit) King (1943-   )
American. First sportwoman to earn more than $100,000 in one year. Holder of twenty Wimbledon titles for single and doubles play. A major figure in popularizing women's tennis and raising its status vis á vis the men's game.

Donna deVarona (1947-   )
American. Champion swimmer, the world's fastest and best all-around female swimmer during her career. She held 37 individual national titles and won two Olympic gold medals. She is an advocate of women's rights and became the first female television sports commentator.

Peggy Fleming (1948-   )
American. Winner of three consecutive world titles in figure skating and Olympic gold in 1968. Her success and charismatic personality revived the American skating program.

Susan Butcher (1954-   )
American. World's foremost long distance sled-dog racer. She has won the Iditarod 1157-mile sled race four times.

Chris Evert (1954-   )
American. Personified women's professional tennis for two decades before her recent retirement. Her popularity brought the women's pro tennis tour into the mainstream. Holder of 157 singles titles, matching Navratilova's record.

Olga Korbut* (1955-   )
Russian. Original, daring and graceful gymnast who sparked much American interest in gymnastics. Won three gold medals at the 1972 Olympics at the age of 16.

Martina Navratilova* (1956-   )
Czech-American. A controversial figure of immense talent in women's tennis. She led female pro tennis players in incorporating fitness training into her regimen and bore the brunt of criticism about her subsequent "manly" looks. Fitness training is now considered routine. Winner of 157 titles and is tied with Evert for all-time championship wins.

Evelyn Ashford (1957-   )
African-American. The top female sprinter whose career has included medals at four Olympics. She defined women's sprinting in the 1980s.

Nadia Comaneci (1961-   )
Romanian. First gymnast to receive a perfect score of 10 in Olympic competition. Remembered for her delicate looks, strength, and agility. Her popularity inspired many young girls to take up gymnastics. Winner of three overall European titles and four Olympic gold medals.

Jackie Joyner-Kersee* (1962-   )
African-American. Track and field hepathlete(7 events), winner of two Olympic gold medals for heptathlon competition also as well as other Olympic medals and many world records. Rivals Babe Didrikson's unofficial title of best female athlete of all time.

Explorers

There is little encouragement even now for women to venture off on their own, investigating the world. In her own way, each of the women below found the courage to travel into the unknown. Most had the money to finance their expeditions, also.

Mary Kingsley (1862-1900)
British. The first woman to travel unaccompanied by a European male in West Africa. Her expertise on the native culture came from her dealings as a trader; her attitude on colonialism was ahead of its time.

Margery Perham (1895-1982)
British. Perham and her sister were the first white women to live on the border between Somalia and Ethiopia. Perham became an authority on Africa and wrote about British policy in its African colonies.

Anna Louise Strong (1885-1970)
American. Political journalist who spent most of her life in countries which were rapidly changing, notably China. Her writings expressed sympathy with socialist struggles and her last years were spent in China as an honored figure.

Freya Madeline Stark (1893-1989?)
Paris-born Briton. She published extensively on her travels in the Middle East and made her home in Italy.

Grace Gallatin Thompson Seton (1872-1959)
American. An active suffragist who travelled and wrote about Asia and South America, as well as the American West and Europe. Her special interest was woman's status.

Dervla Murphy (1931-   )
Irish. She biked through Europe, the Middle East, India, Tibet, and South America and is known for authoring entertaining books about her travels.

Alexandra David-Neel (1868-1969)
French. Journalist, scholar and traveller. The first Western woman to venture into Tibet's forbidden city, Lhasa. She made the journey disguised as a beggar and pilgrim, accompanied by a young male llama whom she later adopted. She wrote about Tibetan life and religion.

Ynes Enriquetta Julietta Mexia (1870-1938)
Mexican-American. A fearless adventurer and botanical explorer travelling through South America, Mexico, and Alaska.

Louise Arner Boyd* (1887-1972)
American. The first woman to fly over the North Pole. She planned, headed, and financed seven expeditions into the Arctic. A portion of Greenland is named Louise Boyd Land in her honor.

Amelia Earhart (1898-1937)
American. Aviator, lecturer/writer on aviation, and national hero. The first woman to fly the Atlantic solo.

Jacqueline Cochran (1910-1980)
American. Holder of more speed records than any other female aviator.
First woman to break the sound barrier.

Jacqueline Auriol (Marie-Thérèse Suzanne Douet) (1917-)
French. The world's first female test pilot, among the first to break the sound barrier and to fly the Concorde.

Krystyna Chojnowska-Liskiewicz (1936-)
Polish. Yachtswoman and the first woman to sail around the world solo(March 1976-March 1978). She works as a shipbuilding engineer.

Valentina Tereshkova (1937-)
Russian. Aerospace engineer and the first woman in space(1963).

Junko Tabei (1939-)
Japanese. The first female mountaineer to reach the top of Mount Everest.
She led an all-woman expedition.

Sally Ride (1951-)
American. Scientist, astronaut and the first American woman in space. She has become a leading advocate of greater scientific opportunities for women.

"Far north, hidden behind grim barriers of pack ice, are lands that hold one spellbound. Gigantic imaginary gates, with hinges set in the horizon, seem to guard these lands. Slowly the gates swing open, and one enters another world where men are insignificant amid the awesome immensity of lonely mountains, fiords, and glaciers."

Louise Arner Boyd*
The Fiord Region of East Greenland, 1935

"Some day I shall go down by the route of the great deserts to China! Some day I shall strike south over the Khyber Pass to India! Some day I shall go by the world's highest mountains and most secret wastes, traveling with the nomads in the heart of Asia!"

Anna Louise Strong*
The Road to the Grey Pamir, 1931

Benchmarks in Sports

1874 Mary Ewing Outerbridge introduces lawn tennis to America.

1889 US Lawn Tennis Association(USLTA) officially permits women to compete.

1895 First US Golf Association Women's Amateur Tournament.

1895 Annie Smith Peck scales the Matterhorn at age 45.

1896 First intercollegiate basketball competition for women.

1905 May Sutton becomes the first American woman to win Wimbledon.

1908 Women permitted to compete officially in the Olympics for the first time in figure skating, gymnastics, swimming and diving events. The American Olympic Committee does not allow American women to compete.

1911 Kate Sandivina lifts 286 pounds, a record which stands until 1985.

1914 Amateur Athletic Union(AAU) sanctions swimming and diving events for women and in 1916, some track and field events.

1920 American women permitted into Olympic competition.

1931 Virne "Jackie" Mitchell signs with the all-male baseball team the Chattanooga Lookouts and, in an exhibition game with the Yankees, strikes out Babe Ruth and Lou Gerhig.

1931 Most college educators believe intercollegiate competition is harmful to women. Only 12% of 227 colleges polled allow such events. The all-black Tuskegee Institute is a notable exception. Athletic director Cleveland Abbott promotes track and field for both genders.

1937 First sanctioned American championship bicycle race for women.

1937 Tuskegee Institute's women's track team wins the AAU championship and continues to do so for 10 of the next 11 years. Teams include future Olympic star Wilma Rudolph* and other world-class athletes.

1943 All-American Girls Baseball League formed to attract fans to the ballpark until World War II was over and male players returned. Each team had a chaperone. Six hundred women compete between 1943 and 1954. Their story is resurrected nearly fifty years later in the film, *A League of Their Own*(1992).

1949 Ladies Professional Golf Association(LPGA)* formed.

1950 Althea Gibson* breaks the color barrier in women's tennis by competing in the US National Championships.

1953 Maureen Connolly* becomes the first woman to win the Grand Slam of Tennis(winning the American, British, French, and Australian Opens in a single year).

1956 "Babe" Didrikson Zaharias* loses her battle with cancer. She rivals Jim Thorpe for greatest American athlete.

1957 Women's intercollegiate competition finally is addressed in earnest by the reconstituted Division for Girls' and Women's Sports(DGWS).

1960 The Olympics are carried for the first time via satellite and millions of Americans watch track star Wilma Rudolph* win gold.

1967 Committee on Intercollegiate Athletics for Women is formed by the DGWS and national championships are instituted.

1970 Women's athletics receives 1% of total college athletic budgets.

1971 Virginia Slims cigarettes provides $100,000 to sponsor the women's tennis tour.

1972 Title IX* outlaws sex discrimination. Participation in female interscholastic athletics jumps 616% between 1971 and 1982.

1972 Boston Marathon establishes a Women's Division after repeated attempts by women runners to join the race.

1972 Russian Olympic gymnast Olga Korbut inspires a generation of American gymnasts.

1973 A women's professional track and field tour becomes reality.

1981-2 125,000+ women compete in events sponsored by the Association of Intercollegiate Athletics for Women(AIAW).

1982 Women's athletics receives 20% of total college athletic budgets, an increase of 1900% since 1970. Participation in the same period climbs 150%.

1982 AIAW loses a battle to prevent the NCAA from sponsoring tournaments. The NCAA didn't include women until the 1980s, while all-woman events have existed since 1967.

1986 National Women in Sports Day established(February 7).

1988 317 American women compete in the Calgary Olympics, along with 1128 men.

1990 35,000+ play on women's softball team.

1991 Kraft sponsors the women's tennis tour with $24 million.

1992 Jackie Joyner-Kersee* wins her second Olympic hepathlon gold. She is acclaimed as the greatest female athlete in the world.

"The moment I stepped out onto that crunchy red clay, felt the grit under my sneakers, felt the joy of smacking the ball over the net, I knew I was in the right place."
Martina Navratilova*

If I could hunt the open fields,
Or march to war, a soldier tall,
If heaven listened to my plea,
Made me a man, even though small!
Instead, I sit here-delicate,
Polite, precise, well-mannered child.
Dreams shake my loosened hair—the wind
Lone listener to my spirit wild.
Annette von Droste-Hülshoff*
From *"On the Tower"*

I want to be a real cowboy girl,
And wear all the buckles and straps,
And know how it feels to have spurs on my heels,
Then strut about in my chaps.
I want to wear a ten-gallon hat,
And a belt that is four inches wide,
Then bulldog a steer at the fair every year
And jump on my pony and ride.
From *"I Want to Be a Real Cowboy Girl"*
Words & music by Mildred and Dorothy Good, c.1930

You never get nothing
By being an angel child,
You better change your ways
And get real wild.
I want to tell you something
I wouldn't tell you no lie,
Wild women are the only kind
That really get by,
'Cause wild women don't worry,
Wild women don't have the blues.
From *"Wild Women Blues"*
Words by Ida Cox, c. 1930

A Heritage of My Own

" The history of every country begins in the heart of a man or woman. "
Willa Cather
O Pioneers! 1913

A Personal Heritage

You've read about your female ancestors "at large." Now here's a chance to record information about yourself and your very own female ancestors. Because the **Scrapbook** *centers on appreciating the women in our past and present, we've kept the same focus for the personal heritage section below. For those who wish to include other female or male relatives or friends, there is plenty of blank space to customize your life and times and the heritage which is yours alone.*

I was born on _____ at _____ o'clock in _____

My full name is _____

I was named after _____

Here's what I know about my birth:

I was the _____ girl in a family of _____

My close family includes:

My Mother

My mother was born on _____ at _____
(place)

She was _____ years old when I was born.

My mother grew up in _____ and lived as an adult in _____

My mother's education consisted of

As a girl, my mother wanted to be _____ when she grew up.

My mother works/worked as a

Her social/community activities are/were

Her religion is/was

My mother is/was particularly good at

She is/was awful when it came to

My mother loves/loved to spend time

She hates/hated to spend time

She reads/read

My mother loved to enjoy these artistic, cultural or media experiences:

Her closest companions are/were

My mother taught me

My Grandmothers

My maternal grandmother is/was _____ *, born* _____
She lives/lived in these settings:

Her racial/ethnic background is/was

Here's what I know about my grandmother's life:

My paternal grandmother is/was _____ *, born* _____

She lived in these settings:

Her racial/ethnic background is/was

Here's what I know about my grandmother's life:

I know these things about my greatgrandmothers:

My Childhood

I was close to these family members:

We used to play at

My favorite plaything was

Family activities included:

My favorite spot in our home was

The things I loved to do most were

The special times I recall in our home were

Our religious or cultural activities included

I have especially fond memories of

My worst memory of childhood is

I was very good at

I was terrible at

When I grew up, I wanted to be

My most precious possessions were

My favorite books were

My first movie I remember is

My special friends were

The adults I looked up to most were

I first menstruated at _____ years. Here's what I remember about it:

My favorite places to be were

My Adolescence

I started my formal education at age ___ and it ended at age ___.
The schools I attended were

My favorite subject in school was

The subject(s) I hated was/were

The teachers I liked best were

My best/worst memory of a teacher is

My best friends through school were

I was successful at

I was lousy at

The most memorable experience I had in school was

I spent my time as a teenager doing things like

My heroes were

My special place as a teen was

The artistic, cultural, and media experiences I loved best were

When I compared myself to other young women, I felt

My first job for hire was

My duties included

My first romantic experience was

My first sexual experience was

I came to realize what my life's work would be in this way:

The pivotal experience of my adolescence was

My Adulthood

As I grew to adulthood, I changed in these ways:

My heroes became

I've lived in these settings as an adult:

As an adult, I've come to love different things and experiences. For example,

I like to spend time doing

I hate to spend time

I've travelled to

The artistic, cultural, and media experiences I enjoy most are

My favorite indoor and outdoor activities are

The people who constitute my family are

I enjoy these activities with them:

My most memorable times with family are

My special friends in adulthood are/have been

My fondest memories with friends are

I've held these jobs:

I consider my life's work to be

It is satisfying to me because

I don't like about it that

I give back to my community by

Here's what I really like about my life:

What I'd like to change is

112

Sources for Further Reading

Please refer to the text for sources not listed below.

Albers, Patricia and Medicine, Beatrice, eds. *The Hidden Half: Studies of Plains Indian Women.* University Press of America, 1983.

Adelaide, Debra. *Australian Women Writers: A Bibliographic Guide.* Pandora(Sydney), 1988.

Alic, Margaret. *Hypatia's Heritage: A History of Women in Science from Antiquity through the Nineteenth Century.* Beacon, 1986.

Ashton, Dore, and Hare, Denise Browne. *Rosa Bonheur: A Life and Legend.* Viking, 1981.

Bernikow, Louise,ed. *The World Split Open: Four Centuries of Women Poets in England and America, 1552-1950.* Vintage, 1974.

Bowers, Jane and Tick, Judith, eds. *Women Making Music: The Western Art Tradition, 1150-1950.* University of Illinois, 1986.

Broker, Ignatia. *Night Flying Woman.* Minnesota Historical Society, 1982.

Broude, Norma and Garrard, Mary D., eds. *Feminism and Art History: Questioning the Litany.* Icon, 1982.

Buhle, Mari Jo and Paul. *The Concise History of Woman Suffrage: Selections from the Classic Work of Stanton, Anthony, Gage and Harper.* University of Illinois, 1978.

Carson, Rachel. *The Sea Around Us.* Oxford University, 1951.

Chicago, Judy. *Through the Flower: My Struggle as an Artist.* Anchor, 1975.

Clark, Judith Freeman. *Almanac of American Women in the 20th Century.* Prentice-Hall, 1987.

Cohen, Aaron I. *International Encyclopedia of Women Composers.* 2d ed. Books and Music, 1987.

Cosman, Carol, Keefe, Joan, and Weaver, Kathleen, eds. *The Penguin Book of Women Poets.* Penguin, 1978.

Dahl, Linda. *Stormy Weather: The Music and Lives of a Century of Jazz Women.* Pantheon, 1984.

Erro-Peralta, Nora and Silva-Nuñez, Caridad, eds. *Beyond the Border: A New Age in Latin American Women's Fiction.* Cleis, 1991.

Forster, Margaret. *Significant Sisters: The Grassroots of Active Feminism, 1839-1939.* Knopf, 1984.

Garrard, Mary D. *Artemisia Gentileschi: The Image of the Female Hero in Italian Baroque Art.* Princeton University, 1989.

Garrow, David, ed. *The Montgomery Bus Boycott and the Women Who Started It: The Memoir of JoAnn Gibson Robinson.* University of Tennessee, 1987.

Giddings, Paula. *When and Where I Enter: The Impact of Black Women on Race and Sex in America.* William Morrow, 1984.

Gilbert, Sandra and Gubar, Susan. *The Norton Anthology of Women's Literature: The Tradition in British.* Norton, 1985.??

Gordon, Linda. *Woman's Body, Woman's Right: A Social History of Birth Control in America.* Grossman, 1976.

Hall, Jacquelyn Dowd. *Revolt Against Chivalry: Jessie Daniel Ames and the Women's Campaign Against Lynching.* Columbia University, 1979.

Haskell, Molly. *From Reverence to Rape:The Treatment of Women in The Movies.* 2d ed. Univ. of Chicago, 1987.

Hayden, Dolores. *The Grand Domestic Revolution: A History of Feminist Design for American Homes, Neighborhoods and Cities.* MIT, 1981.

Heck-Rabi, Louise. *Women Filmmakers: A Critical Reception.* Scarecrow Press, 1984.

Hepworth, Barbara. *A Pictorial Autobiography.* Moonraker Press, 1978.

Hoff, Joan Wilson. *Law, Gender, and Injustice: A Legal History of U.S. Women.* NYU, 1991.

Holcomb, Mabs and Wood, Sharon. *Deaf Women: A Parade Through the Decades.* Dawn Sign, 1989.

Holiday, Billie, with William Duffy. *Lady Sings the Blues.* Lancer, 1956.

Holt, Barbara. *Terrible Perfection: Women and Russian Literature.* Indiana University, 1987.

Jacobs, Mary Jane. *Magdelena Abakanowicz.* Abbeville Press, 1989.

James, Adeola. *In Their Own Voices: African Women Writers Talk.* American publisher: Heinemann, 1990.

Jhabvala, Ruth Prawer. *Heat and Dust.* Harper & Row, 1975.

Jones, Mary Harris. *The Autobiography of Mother Jones.* 3rd ed. Kerr, 1976.

Kass-Simon G. and Farnes, Patricia. *Women of Science: Righting the Record.* Indiana University, 1990.

Kersey, Ethel M. *Women Philosophers: A Bio-Critical Source Book.* 1989.

Lindstrom, Naomi. *Women's Voice in Latin American Literature.* Three Continents, 1989.

Lisle, Laurie. *Portrait of an Artist: A Biography of Georgia O'Keeffe.* Pocketbooks, 1987.

Macdonald, Anne L. *Feminine Ingenuity: Women and Invention in America.* Ballantine, 1992.

Mathews, Nancy Mowll. *Cassatt and Her Circle: Selected Letters.* Abbeville Press, 1984.

Morantz-Sanchez, Regina Markell. *Sympathy and Science: Women Physicians in American Medicine.* Oxford University, 1985.

Morgan, Robin. *Sisterhood is Global: The International Women's Movement Anthology.* Anchor, 1984.

Nichols, Victoria and Thompson, Susan. *Silk Stalkings: When Women Write of Murder.* Black Lizard, 1988.

Olsen, Tillie. *Silences.* Dell, 1978.

Rossi, Alice. *The Feminist Papers: From Adams to de Beauvoir.* Columbia University, 1973.

Rossiter, Margaret. *Women Scientists in America: Struggles and Strategies to 1940.* Johns Hopkins, 1982.

Sarton, Eva Martin and Zimmerman, Dorothy Wayne, eds. *French Women Writers: A Bio-Bibliographical Source Book.* Greenwood, 1991.

Sayre, S. *Rosalind Franklin and DNA.* W.W. Norton, 1975.

Schiebinger, Londa. *The Mind Has No Sex? Women in the Origins of Modern Science.* Harvard University, 1989.

Schlobin, Roger C. *Urania's Daughters: A Checklist of Women Science Fiction Writers, 1692-1982.* Starmont House, 1973.

Seager, Joni and Olson, Ann. *Women in the World: An International Atlas.* Touchstone, 1986.

Shockley, Ann Allen. *Afro-American Women Writers, 1746-1933.* G. K. Hall, 1988.

Slatkin, Wendy. *Women Artists in History: From Antiquity to the 20th Century.* 2d ed. Prentice Hall, 1990.

Sparhawk, Ruth M. et al. *American Women in Sport, 1887-1987.* Scarecrow, 1989.

Spender, Dale, ed. *The Penguin Anthology of Australian Women's Writing.* Penguin, 1988.

Stevens, Doris. *Jailed for Freedom: The Story of the Militant American Suffragist Movement.* Schocken, 1976.

Tinling, Marion. *Women into the Unknown: A Sourcebook on Women Explorers and Travellers.* Greenwood, 1989.

Tinling, Marion. *Women Remembered: A Guide to Landmarks of Women's History in the United States.* Greenwood Press, 1986.

Wald, Lillian. *The House on Henry Street.* Holt, 1915.

Walker, Alice. *In Search of Our Mothers' Gardens.* Harcourt Brace Jovanovich, 1983.

Watanabe, Sylvia and Bruchac, Carol. *Home to Stay: Asian American Women's Fiction.* Greenfield Review, 1990.

Wenner, Hilda E. and Freilicher, Elizabeth. *Here's to the Women: 100 Songs for and about American Women.* Syracuse University, 1987.

Williams, Barbara. *Breakthrough: Women in Archaeology.* Walker, 1981.

Zahniser, J. D. *And Then She Said: Quotations by Women for Every Occasion.* 2 vols. Caillech Press, 1989 & 1990.